John Cookson

Hannibal and Katharna

A drama in five acts

John Cookson

Hannibal and Katharna
A drama in five acts

ISBN/EAN: 9783337317935

Printed in Europe, USA, Canada, Australia, Japan

Cover: Foto ©Thomas Meinert / pixelio.de

More available books at **www.hansebooks.com**

CONTENTS

		PAGE
PREFACE	. . . .	v
DRAMATIS PERSONÆ	. . . .	ix
ACT I. SCENE 1	. . . .	1
Yahwa's " Song of the Oriole"	. . . .	9
ACT I. SCENE 2	. . . . . .	1c
,, 3	. . . . .	1ɛ
,, 4	. . . .	31
,, 5	. . . .	4ɩ
,, 6	. . . .	4ɩ
ACT II. SCENE 1	. . . .	5ɩ
,, 2	. . . .	6ɩ
,, 3	. . . .	7
,, 4	. . . .	8
,, 5	. . . .	8
ACT III. SCENE 1	. . . . . .	9
,, 2	. . . .	9
,, 3	. . . .	9
,, 4	. . . .	ç
,, 5	. . . . .	1c
,, 6	. . . .	1c

viii   CONTENTS

		PAGE
ACT IV. SCENE 1 .		115
,, 2 .		120
,, 3 .		128
,, 4 .		135
,, 5 .		144
,, 6		148
ACT V. SCENE 1 .		152
,, 2 .		163
Yahwa's " Song of the Caged Bird "		164
ACT V. SCENE 3		177
,, 4		182
,, 5		186

DRAMATIS PERSONÆ

HAMILCAR . . . *The famous Carthaginian General and Suffete.*

HANNIBAL . . .⎫
HASDRUBAL . . ⎬ *His Sons : all Carthaginian Generals.*
MAGO . . . . ⎭

MAGDASSAN . . { *A Carthaginian General: Second-in-Command of Hamilcar's army in Spain.*

GISCO . . . . *Chief of the Staff of Hannibal's armies.*

MAHARBAL . . *A General in command of Hannibal's Cavalry.*

BASILIO . . . . *A Nobleman of ancient Spain.*

KATHARNA.
ALALIA . . . } *His Daughters.*

HERCTA. . . . *Their Attendant.*

HANNO . . . { *A Carthaginian Suffete: leader of the faction opposed to Hamilcar and his family.*

MALCHUS . . *His confidential Agent.*

ABDALONIM . . *An Agent of Malchus.*

MUTHUMBAL . . *A Carthaginian Scribe.*

YAHWA . . . { *Hamilcar's Minstrel: afterwards in the service of Kings Sphax and Massinissa.*

SCIPIO . . . . *The Roman General, surnamed "Africanus."*

ELISSA . . . { *Widow of a Carthaginian General, of the faction opposed to Hanno.*

SOPHONISBA . . *Her young and beautiful Daughter.*

ix

KING SPHAX . . } *Rival African Princes ruling maritime states to*
KING MASSINISSA } *the West of Carthage.*

PARIHU . . . . { *Chief Officer of the Palace to King Sphax, and*
{ *afterwards to King Massinissa.*

THE HUNCHBACK { *A Jester at the Court of King Sphax, and after-*
{ *wards at that of King Massinissa.*

THE HIGH PRIEST OF JUPITER.

AULUS . . . . } *Roman Soldiers.*
GAVIUS . . . }

Senators, Ambassadors, Courtiers, Officers, Augurs, Magicians, Messengers, Soldiers, Civilians, Trumpeters, Insurgents, Slaves, &c.

HANNIBAL AND KATHARNA

ACT I.

SCENE I.

*The Carthaginian camp in Spain during foot-races and
games. The course traverses the front of the stage,
and behind it stand crowds of soldiers looking on;
in the centre, among the spectators, is a tent, at the
door of which a standard is planted.*

FIRST SOLDIER.

What distance do they go this time?

SECOND SOLDIER.

A mile:
And there they sally now around the bend,
Their racing legs resembling wheels!

FIRST SOLDIER.

Hah! hah!
A strange idea of yours, to run on wheels,
As one might ride a horse; but there they come.
Who, think you, wins the race?

SECOND SOLDIER.

The swiftest man :
No demon sits astride upon his neck
To hold him back and rob him of the prize !

(*The runners pass, amidst excited shouts from
the crowd.*)

Well run ! well run !   Already now they start
The second race : there falls the signal flag.

(*Enter* MUTHUMBAL. *He is stoutish, panting from
the heat, and holds his helmet in his hand, while
mopping his face with a handkerchief.*)

Well met, Muthumbal : do *you* run to-day ?

MUTHUMBAL.

Why, only as you see : 'tis very hot !

SECOND SOLDIER.

Come, tell us now : how many Roman heads
Were gathered after yester's skirmishing ?

MUTHUMBAL (*aside*).

He is inquisitive, and greatly lacks
That keen respect which should be due to me ;
I'll put him off with quips and tell nothing,
Until the list is published in the camp ;

(*Knowingly.*)

Let us bamboozle the inquisitive !

(*Aloud.*)

Well, answer then another question first :

Tell me how many Roman soldiers' helms
Were emptied by it ?

SECOND SOLDIER (*aside*).

         True, I am no scribe,
And yet I'll show that I'm as sharp as he !

                      (*Aloud.*)

Many a good Roman parted with his helm,
But being dead had little want of it ;
Although I know a man not far from here,
Without a helmet, who has lost his head :
And, being still alive, he needs them much.

    (MUTHUMBAL *moves away muttering and putting on
       his helmet. The runners in the second race pass,
       amid cheers. Enter two Soldiers who ran in the
       second race, and now dispute the prize.*)

FIRST RUNNER (*angrily*).

Come to the judge and hear what justice says !

        (*Addressing an Officer who is standing near
                   the flag.*)

I pray Magdassan may decide our cause.

        (*The Officer enters the tent, and returns, pre-
            ceded by* MAGDASSAN.)

FIRST RUNNER (*to* MAGDASSAN).

Most honoured Chief, he crossed me at the turn,
Or I had won !

SECOND RUNNER.

My Lord, his words are false ;
In fact, he slipped upon the scorched-up ground,
And almost threw me down !

(*To the* FIRST RUNNER.)

Let's fight it out,
Like men, to-morrow morning at the dawn !

MAGDASSAN.

Have patience both, nor idly waste good blood :
Fight only with the foe, and then strive well.
You say you are the fastest ?

FIRST RUNNER.

Aye, my Lord.

MAGDASSAN.

And you claim greater speed ?

SECOND RUNNER.

Yes, noble sir.

MAGDASSAN.

Then it would be a boon to both of you
To run again and better prove your worth.
So I decide.   This evening let it be.

(*Exeunt the Runners. A flourish of trumpets is
heard.* MAGDASSAN *continues, addressing the
soldiers.*)

My sons, our mighty leader will arrive,
To join your sports, as he has shared your toils ;
I need not ask that you should greet the Chief
Most reverently : and now Hamilcar comes !

(*Enter* HAMILCAR, *preceded by trumpeters and an
armed escort. He is attended by* HANNIBAL,
HASDRUBAL, GISCO, YAHWA, &c. *The soldiers
bow the head as* HAMILCAR *passes them : they then
remain erect and facing toward him.* HAMILCAR
*takes his place in front of the standard : the trum-
peters and escort draw up on his right, and the staff
on his left. The trumpeters sound a flourish, at
the end of which the whole concourse of soldiers
salute* HAMILCAR *by bowing the head and bending
the knee : he acknowledges the salute by extending
his right hand towards them, first to the right and
then to the left ; the staff then breaks up its ranks,
the soldiers resume their occupations, the trumpeters
and escort march to the back of the scene, where
they remain drawn up, awaiting orders. Enter
at one extremity of the scene, behind the lines of
soldier-spectators,* BASILIO, *leaning on a stick : next,
on his further side, and slightly behind, comes*
KATHARNA, *leading by the hand* ALALIA, *who
appears to shrink timidly back :* HANNIBAL *observes them and approaches, then stops.*)

HANNIBAL (*aside*).

What beauty, youth, and innocence are here !
I will approach awhile to sun myself
In their bright presence ; and indeed I feel
There might be more to charm in Spain at peace
Than I had fancied.
> (*Addressing the Soldiers in front of* BASILIO.)
                    Soldiers, clear a space
For welcome visitors.
> (*The Soldiers obey.*)

BASILIO.

                    I thank you, sir.
What Cathaginian leader honours me,
With courtesy to one so old and worn ?

HANNIBAL.

My name is Hannibal.   May I inquire
Your noble house of Spain ?

BASILIO.

                    Alas, my Lord,
Although my garb claims rank, my fortunes ebb ;
Our lands and wealth were lost in civil wars,
The curse of Spain.   I own a long descent
From the bold ruler of the Western coast,
Who triumphed in Iberia's sacred cause
Against invasions of the fiery Gaul,
Despoiler of our land upon the East.
My name's Basilio : at your service, sir.

HANNIBAL.

And I at yours, my Lord, with all my heart !
(*He looks at* KATHARNA, *who lowers her eyes.*)
But pray excuse me for a moment, sir.

(HANNIBAL *returns to* HAMILCAR *and
addresses him.*)

HANNIBAL.

Now there are easy opportunities
To flatter noble Spain through one of rank,
Basilio, who is present with his friends.
Pray show him favour.

HAMILCAR.

Certainly, my son :
The chance may serve us well.   I wish to learn
The hopes and fears of Spaniards for the war.
Conduct him hither presently.

HANNIBAL.

I will.

(HANNIBAL *returns to* BASILIO *and
addresses him.*)

HANNIBAL.

My father, sir, requests your company,
Where you may best observe the soldiers' games ;
I pray you follow where Hamilcar waits.

(BASILIO, KATHARNA, *and* ALALIA *follow* HANNI-
BAL *to the standard, where* HAMILCAR *greets them
most courteously, and converses with* BASILIO ;
while HANNIBAL *talks with* KATHARNA, *who still
holds* ALALIA'S *hand.*)

HAMILCAR (*to* BASILIO).

My Lord, you are by right our host in Spain,
And we your guests.   Thrice welcome to my camp !
I hope you may return to visit me
Whene'er you wish to treat of politics :
Learning my latest news from Africa,
Or favouring me with yours on home affairs :
To pass a pleasant hour.

BASILIO.

                    Accept my thanks :
Your Excellency honours me indeed !

HAMILCAR.

See, Yahwa, there's an oriole on the tree :
Now tune your lay to match his carolling.

(YAHWA *steps forward, looks up at the bird, and strikes
a few chords on his guitar : he then sings to its ac-
companiment, smiling and playfully addressing the
bird.*)

SONG OF THE ORIOLE.

I.

An oriole flutters on a bough,
  Singing in praise of the cherries :
" They're not yet ripe, but are ripening now,
  Those lovely, luscious berries !

II.

" I fought through winter with the cold,
  Famine, rain, wind, and the thunder :
But now I'm here, and my tale is told,
  My frame nigh riven asunder !

III.

" The stormy season past, I've come
  Home to my haunts in the valley :
Where warmly shines the reviving sun,
  And whispering zephyrs tarry.

IV.

" Here will I warble notes of love,
  Flute-like, resonant, and mellow ;
Nest in the branch of a pine-wood grove,
  With a mate all black and yellow.

V.

" Yes, Summer brings me back again,
    Over the waters from Zelies :
Cherries are ripening fast in Spain,
    Those lovely, luscious berries !

VI.

" So here I flutter on the bough,
    Chanting the charms of the cherries :
They'll soon be ripe, and are ripening now,
    Those lovely, luscious berries ! "

                       (*Curtain.*)

Scene II.

BASILIO'S *Homestead.*   *Enter* ALALIA *and* HERCTA.

ALALIA.

When did you hear this ?

HERCTA.

           Madam, only now :
I chanced to meet a shepherd from the hill,
Who said that as he reached the highest crest
He saw the Romans move to cross the stream ;
Long columns met and waded through the ford,

While others in broad barges ferried o'er
Where it was deep ; then opposite the isle
Some hardy horsemen plunged into the waves,
And gallantly attained the sandy wharf
That lies midway : they rested there awhile,
Then safely swam across the further arm.
But as the shepherd hastened down again,
Driving his flocks, as ordered, to the fold,
Still other troops approached the crossing-points,
While scattered on the further river-bank
There streamed great toiling crowds upon the slopes ;
Entering the thickest forests on the brows,
Towards the rocky passes in the hills,
As if to cross, or halt upon the range
Within the woodlands.

ALALIA.

                    Most important news :
Those troops may now be on their way from Spain,
To leave us once again in grateful peace ;
And when they gain their homes in Italy,
What joy must kindle in the anxious breasts
Of wives and children for their safe return !
And Carthage will feel equal happiness
At the home-coming of her well-loved sons.

HERCTA (*hastily*).

But will *they* leave us too ?

ALALIA.

Of course !   Why not ?

HERCTA (*thoughtfully*).

Only that they are gallant men indeed,
And their protection gives security.

ALALIA.

But when the danger has all passed away,
What need for shield and weapons ?

HERCTA (*coquettishly*).

None, 'tis true :
Unless worn as an ornamental badge,
To please the fancy in our leisure hours.

ALALIA.

But women need no trophy of the kind !

HERCTA (*archly*).

There may be no necessity ; and yet
Some prize it all the more for that.

ALALIA (*smiling*).

Indeed ?
Well, Hercta, if the highly-tempered blade
Must now be stored in distant armouries,
I trust its glitter may not draw you hence ;
But rather, if it be of sterling worth,

That you will stay and keep it by your side :
I hope that all may prosper.

HERCTA (*dubiously*).

Ah, madam !
'Tis sad to part from such a faithful friend.

ALALIA.

Who may he be ?

HERCTA (*simply*).

Muthumbal is his name :
A scribe on duty with the Punic host.

ALALIA (*hesitating*).

I thought you said he was a warrior :
Or from your words I might infer as much ?

HERCTA (*pettishly*).

His heart beats high with martial energy,
Yet somebody must do the writing part !
                 (*A pause, during which* HERCTA *frets with
                          evident annoyance.*)
Indeed, his post is most responsible :
Your father says one scribe who wields a pen
Can do more harm than fifty men with swords !
                          (*Another similar pause.*)
Besides, he ranks as captain of a troop !
                          (*A similar pause.*)

ALALIA.

What are his functions?

HERCTA (*proudly*).

Registering the heads
Struck from the fallen foes throughout the war.

ALALIA (*aside*).

Most barbarous work!

(*Aloud.*)
How did you chance to meet?

HERCTA (*naively*).

One day he passed when I was at the gate,
And, pausing, asked most courteously of me
The homestead's name, for note upon his maps:

(*A pause.*)
Since then he takes his evening walks this way.

ALALIA.

Where can I view from some convenient point
The Roman host, and verify the tale
Told by the shepherd?

HERCTA.

Madam, follow me
To where a recent clearing in the wood,
Upon the steepest slopes below us here,
Pierces the woven leafy curtain through:
And there you can observe the Roman troops.

ALALIA.

Lead on, good Hercta, I will follow you.

(*Exeunt.*)

Enter HANNIBAL *and* KATHARNA.

HANNIBAL.

Katharna, you control my happiness :
So move your father most judiciously
To gain his full consent, and without fail.
Discreetly mention that I value high
His noble blood, that tells of glorious deeds,
Which ornament a country's history :
And, tingling in his bold descendant's veins,
Will give sure promise of success to come.
So when we meet at midday I shall learn
With how much favour he regards my suit.
My heart is in your tender keeping, love.

KATHARNA.

Believe me, dear, no keen ambassador
Had e'er a policy that touched him more,
In his own tenderness and interests,
Than ours moves me.

(*Exit* HANNIBAL : *then enter* BASILIO
from the house.)

KATHARNA.

Dear father, I'll confess
A secret known as yet to only two.

BASILIO (*laughing*).

'Twill soon be spread abroad by one of us !
This is my way of looking on the case :
I hold a secret, as a sword, alone,
Grasping the easy hilt to balance it,
So I can turn the sabre as I will ;
Another aiding me must seize the blade,
And, the more pungent is the biting edge
The louder will he howl the circumstance ;
But if by chance to join us comes a third,
Of needs he takes the point, which tickles him
Till, laughing, he discloses all he knows.

KATHARNA.

It matters little whether it be told,
If you approve.

BASILIO.

'Tis something serious ;
I thought it was the purchase of a gown
That was desired, and I was wished to pay :
Or promised coming of some welcome guest ;
But now I fancy it is something more.
What is the kernel of the mystery
On which you wish my judgment ?

KATHARNA.

It is this :
During some little while, as you have seen,
Lord Hannibal has sought my company ;

Until to-day he told me of his love,
And prayed me quickly to prepare you, sir :
As he proposed to wait upon you here,
Seeking your sanction to our union.

BASILIO.

Yet, how can Hannibal find time to wed
Amidst campaigns of wild uncertainty,
All seeming endless ?

KATHARNA.

Then, he bade me say :
That from the latest information gained,
The dawn of peace in Spain is close at hand.

BASILIO.

To seal your happiness, I will consent
To it.

KATHARNA.

I thank you, father, heartily.
(*She kisses him.*)
And now I go to meet Lord Hannibal,
Who will be full of joy to hear your words.
(BASILIO *re-enters the house. Exit* KATHARNA.)

SCENE III.

A forest near the Carthaginian camp in Spain.   Enter
HAMILCAR *and* HASDRUBAL.

HAMILCAR (*proudly*).

I have ordained : to-morrow will be drawn,
In battle order, all the forces ranged
As far as eye can reach : a grand review
In honour of our triumph o'er the foe,
And the delivery of fair Spain at last.
Then will I dedicate auspiciously
My eldest son, the skilful Hannibal—
The worthy offspring of a sire who first
Has checked the arms of ever-conquering Rome—
To sacrifice his life opposing her,
And lead our troops to vanquish Italy :
A boon I must forego through stress of years.
At a stone altar in the centre, raised
To mighty Baal-Hammon, shall he swear,
With votive oaths, eternal hate of Rome,
While I as priest will consecrate his vows.
To you I grant a post of equal rank
And vital import to our sovereignty :
No less its honourable dangers loom,
Although it is a stationary command :
For rocky cliffs upon the battered coast
Withstand far more of stormy buffetings
Than swiftly-moving barques that skim the waves.
Your duty is to rule the rich and great

Sea-bordered province of Emporia,
Which still is torn by fierce civil war,
Since Spendius and Matho raised the bands—
In parricidal strife against our power—
Of mercenaries who had fought for us :
Stirring the bile of seething discontent
Amongst the native tribes, which rose in arms,
And still rage in rebellion unsubdued,
Threatening to join the ready foes within,
And by invasion overrun your realm ;
While the wild Eastern hordes which have engulfed
The rich Egyptian valley of the Nile,
With appetites aroused but unappeased,
Prepare themselves beyond our territory
To first assail us at your new command.
Nor is its government less weighty work
Than to lead on the force invading Rome,
That might be vanquished without jeopardy
To Carthage, which would rest secure at home ;
But if Emporia, close beyond our walls,
Successfully defied our utmost power,
And gained her liberty through this revolt,
Then far and near the subject states would rise,
While vaunting Rome might play the deadly game
That we aim at herself in Italy,
And send invading hosts to Africa,
Menacing Carthage on her native soil.

HASDRUBAL (*inclining his head respectfully*).
Your wish, sir, rules both Hannibal and me.

(*Exit* HAMILCAR.)

To-morrow is the day our father holds
The mystic ceremony, which will bind
My brother's life, perhaps for evermore ;

(A pause.)

Such bonds would gall me little : for in heart
I'm free to fight and wonder all my days ;
But Hannibal, who loves so desperately,
Longing for happiness, now Spain is saved,
Could scarcely bear the torture of the blow.

(A pause.)

But then to balk Hamilcar, if resolved :

(A pause.)

Far sooner would I seize, with naked arms,
A lioness in her accustomed cave,
And drag her, roaring, from amongst her cubs !

(A pause.)

I'll save him !

(A pause.)

          Though fate surely marked him out
For open warfare, needing generalship
More than the post our father gives to me,
By breathing in his mind the art of war :
Which makes him far excel, although a youth,
Our captains most experienced in the field.
His name is now a potent talisman
That rouses soldiers to their utmost deed,
Till valour and endurance win the day.

(Enter HANNIBAL.)

HASDRUBAL.

O Hannibal ! I fear the news I bear
Will grieve you much, though I must make it known :

Our father plans to send you on at once,
The master of his hosts, to Italy.

HANNIBAL.

At once !

HASDRUBAL.

Yes, dedicated by a vow—
To-morrow pledged before the gathered troops—
To Moloch's constant service, till the day
When Rome is conquered, Italy subdued.

HANNIBAL.

Alas ! the knell that sounds the certain doom
Of all my earthly happiness, which seemed
Visions too bright for stern reality !
I felt as one who, dreaming, grasps a prize,
Yet, being partly conscious that he sleeps,
Dreads the dull hour when he must wake again,
And it will fade, cheating his eager view ;
Though treasured as a soothing memory,
A sweet remembrance joined with deep regret,
Indelible for ever !

HASDRUBAL.

I conceived
A hastily formed plan to meet the need,
If we enlist our father's sympathy :
That I should take the vow at Moloch's shrine
Instead of you to-morrow, and your part
Would be to save Emporia from the grip

Of deadly foes and demon anarchists—
The duty which our father wills to me.
A lull would come, Emporia's peace restored,
When you might gain domestic happiness,
So much desired.

HANNIBAL (*gloomily*).

Brother, my thanks to you :
Alas ! it cannot be : the fates are stern.
For how could Hannibal place selfish aims
Before his duty to his native land,
His father, and the gods ?   If a mishap
Should meet the army in the snow-clad Alps,
Or in its conflicts with the hardy foes
Who dwell in countries on the destined route,
Or in the deadly shock of arms with Rome,
Carthage might curse my recreant name and say :
The blame is Hannibal's, who in the hour
Of urgent need has failed his country's cause !

HASDRUBAL.

Then, brother, as you will, so let it be.
(*Exit* HASDRUBAL : *then enter* KATHARNA.)

HANNIBAL (*aside*).

She comes : how can I break the mournful news ?

KATHARNA.

Ah, Hannibal ! it is not yet the hour
We fixed upon ; nor would the lagging sands

Run faster for my chiding : so I thought
To be the first to come, but you are here !
I feared you might have gone on urgent work,
Caused by the movements of the Roman force
Which crossed the stream : for so the peasants say.
I heard them as I came discussing it.

(HANNIBAL *kisses her hand with tender respect.*
She observes his gloomy looks.)

Oh, say what news ?

HANNIBAL.

My love, the sunny light
Of your bright face would cheer the darkest day !
But I desire to tell you of a fact
Concerning both of us, and seek advice,
Which you will give so as to guide my steps
With honour in the path of rectitude.
The Roman troops are now in full retreat :
And on the concentration of our force,
My father bids that I should lead his host
To Italy, and thus our union
Of needs must be postponed until the day
When I return here.

KATHARNA (*coaxingly*).

Not till you return.
Come, come, you jest ; or, now I guess the cause :
(*Pettishly.*)
Some fairer face, with brighter eyes than mine.

HANNIBAL.

I am in earnest, and my words are true :
Alas, my love, I would 'twere otherwise !
And of your charms no rivals could be found,
Throughout broad Spain, or on my native coasts
Of Carthage.

KATHARNA.

Hannibal, I pray forgive
My foolish jealousy ; but tell me, dear,
How can we shun this great catastrophe ?

HANNIBAL (*hesitating*).

The destined ruler of Emporia,
My brother, has already offered me
To change our posts : our father's sanction given,
The marriage then might still be possible,
And wedded life amid the cares of rule
Would solace, soothe, and strengthen——

KATHARNA.

Then accept
Pray do this, Hannibal, and rescue me,
Ere yet too late, from terrible despair !
Now reason with me, love, upon the cause :
Say, does the dove that pleads, and not in vain,
Forget his wooing in some distant flight,
Or taste the joys his melody has won ?
How would you bear the absence without words

Of tenderness : or might you soon forget ?
And though I feel that to no other voice
My heart could beat responsively with love,
Would you still hold my troth firm-pledged as now !
(A pause.)

Or death's autumnal blight delay to strike
From off the parent bough neglected fruit
Which lacked too long the gardener's fostering care ?
True instinct whispers me, if once you go
On such a distant arduous enterprise,
That we shall never chance to meet again,
While yet the warmly flowing tide of youth
Invites to present happiness.

HANNIBAL.

My love,
Then I must yield ; for I have not the power
To strive against your wish, nor to deny
The pleadings of my heart.   Now, dearest, wear
The ring I give you as a constant pledge
Of my unchanging love, until you lead
Into a closer, willing servitude
Your firm, devoted slave.
(He places a ring on her finger : she smiles.)

KATHARNA.

A lovely gem
Which I shall ever prize.   I thank you much.
Though little needs my burning heart a breeze
To fan its ardent flame,   My memory

Will never chafe beneath its silken chains,
But ever dwell on you in tenderness.
When, as you wished, I told my father all,
Seeking approval of our marriage vows,
He gladly gave consent to welcome you !

HANNIBAL.

What happiness : I live for you alone !
See now, Hamilcar comes.

KATHARNA.

                    Love, I will go :
So then bespeak your father's grace and aid ;
For if he deems our marriage suitable,
How could he long condemn to live apart
Those whom he judges fit for unity ?

HANNIBAL.

Then let us meet again at eventide,
Upon the threshold of your father's home,
Just at the hour the trumpets sound to mark
The setting of the watch.   Hamilcar's words
I then will bear you : and we will discuss
Our future plans.

KATHARNA.

Yes, dear, let it be so.
(*Exit* KATHARNA : *then enter* HAMILCAR.)

HANNIBAL.

Father, I would converse with you awhile,
If of your goodness you will hear me.

HAMILCAR.

Yes :
Speak on, my son : no better chance appears
For conversation.

HANNIBAL.

Then I ask a boon.
Since childhood I have served in every war :
And as you have commanded, I obeyed.
But now I would request my first reward :
Hasdrubal has unfolded your designs
For both our future enterprises, sir.
Permit that we exchange, for he consents ;
Each war bears equal promise of renown :
Though from the nature of the services,
His being a more sedentary command,
I fain would choose it for a year or two,
That I might woo a lady in the space ;
But when that time is past command again
And send me where you will.

HAMILCAR.

I grant your wish :
Though fiery Moloch in his angry mood,
Aroused by losing thus his votary,
May hinder all your plans whate'er they be.

E'en at your birth I promised you should live
For his high favour : and I named you then,
In token of my wish, " The Grace of Baal."

HANNIBAL.

The risk is mine.   Accept my warmest thanks :
Your words have opened Heaven's gates to me !
I would consult you further on this theme
Of utmost moment : and entreat no less
Than for your weighty sanction to be given
That I may wed.

HAMILCAR.

With whom ?

HANNIBAL.

Katharna, sir
A lady of the noblest blood in Spain,
Although her family, impoverished
Through clannish feuds, lives in a homely way.
You saw her with her father at the sports
And races of our troops, but recently :
Then, while you questioned him to learn the drift
Of Spanish native feeling on the war,
I held communion with her close at hand ;
And now I feel my happiness depends
Upon an early union with her, sir.

HAMILCAR.

I marked you well !   A charming girl, no doubt.
'Tis our hot blood that leads to sudden love,
With great capacity for suffering ;

Yet I would not exchange a single drop
For all the watery fluids filtering
Through the ascetic's cold and fish-like frame !

*(Aside.)

What answer shall I give to his request,
Without offence, yet charged with worldly lore ?
If I forbid him, he'll consider me
The harshest parent in the universe ;
Yet if I grant it, soon a day may come
When he will wish I had denied it him,
Preserving him unfettered from the bond,
And able to pursue his destiny.

(Aloud.)

My son, it is a serious step indeed
That ends your freedom.   Youth loves liberty,
So ponder on it well : then if your wish
Remains unchanged, I will consider it ;
But I had hoped your choice might fall at home,
And that you would have sought to wed, at least,
With a princess of Africa, or else
The daughter of some powerful family
In Carthage.

HANNIBAL.

I have weighed it thoroughly ;
Nor do I hesitate, sir.

HAMILCAR.

Well, my son,
Katharna has consented, I presume :
And do you say Basilio has approved
His daughter's marriage ?

HANNIBAL.

                Yes.   She promised me.
And has disclosed all to her father, sir,
This morning, saying I would come ere long
To seek his blessing if you gave me yours ;
Basilio seemed well pleased and satisfied.

                                  (*Aside.*)

I know what argument will move him most !

                                  (*Aloud.*)

By charms of disposition, face, and form
She has enslaved my heart and judgment, too ;
Being of a mould where nature promises
To generously present a warrior sire
With sturdy offspring suitable for war !

HAMILCAR.

Then I consent, and trust your union
May bring the happiness you have well earned
By long and arduous service in the field.
So, if you have the promised lusty son,
Teach him, as I taught you, to vanquish Rome.
Instruct him in the arts of government,
That haply he may live to rule the world !

HANNIBAL.

I owe much gratitude for your assent,
And highly prize your liberal praise of me,
However poor my merits.

                                  (*Exit* HAMILCAR.)

Haste the hour
That leads me back to dear Katharna's charms :
What joy will then be hers to hear the news,
That I have gained my father's full consent !

(A pause.)

How she is altered since at first we met :
A budding flower then, and now full-blown ;
A tender girl changed to a stately dame.
Love is the sun that ripens womanhood !
Well, I will hasten on the marriage-day :
At least two years of happiness are ours ;
Then if I leave her for the distant wars,
Their memory will prove a talisman
Amid the darkness of adversity ;
And, like a beacon shining through the night,
Will guide and cheer me to success at last.

(Exit.)

Scene IV.

BASILIO'S *homestead.* HERCTA *dusting a table under a tree. Enter* MUTHUMBAL, *passing along a road at the back of the scene : he looks round and nods to* HERCTA, *but moves on doubtfully.*

HERCTA.

There's no one here, Muthumbal : don't be shy !
        (MUTHUMBAL, *who had almost passed out of sight,
        turns smiling, and approaches* HERCTA.)

MUTHUMBAL.

My love, you see I have not failed to come,
As promised.

HERCTA.

I am very glad, indeed :
Welcome, my dear ! I said we are alone.
(*Looks over her shoulder.*)

MUTHUMBAL.

Then I may venture to——
(*He put his arm round* HERCTA'S *waist and, drawing her gently towards him, kisses her cheek.*)

HERCTA (*coyly*).

I meant—not that.

MUTHUMBAL.

'Tis none the worse for coming without thought :
And so I find it.

HERCTA (*pouting*).

Oh, you naughty boy !
I hope naught else may happen unawares—

MUTHUMBAL.

Did time permit and opportunity—

HERCTA (*averting her face for a moment*).
Muthumbal, tell me why you looked so sad
When first you passed the gable ?

MUTHUMBAL (*seriously*).

Well, my dear :
Because the gloomy thought occurred to me,
That I might ne'er again behold this scene,
Rendered so happy by our meetings.

HERCTA.

Why ?

MUTHUMBAL.

The Roman army has abandoned Spain ;
Our troops will not pursue till gathered here,
As lions crouch before they make their spring
To deal a distant blow.   But I return,
Starting to-morrow in the evening,
Charged with the secret archives' custody
Of the late war in Spain, now haply o'er,
To lodge them safe in Carthage.   Then I think
My military work is done at last ;
Unless the Elder's Council should decree
That I must join some other armament :
(*Drawing himself up.*)
Valuing my services already given,
Which, as you know, are neither small nor few ;
But otherwise I must pursue my trade,
As a civilian scribe, in Carthage fixed :
Nor would my humble means enable me
To seek new wanderings round the Punic world.
Now, dear, I pray excuse my hurriedness.

Hercta, 'tis time that I should take my leave,
As business presses much : while there is light.
I pray you walk with me a little way
Towards the camp, that our last interview
May be the longer.

HERCTA.

I half guessed your news.
'Tis sad indeed, Muthumbal, to part thus :
But can we find no remedy ?

MUTHUMBAL.

We'll try ;
Let us discuss it, dear, upon the way :
Your woman's wit is quicker far than mine.
(*Exeunt ; then enter three Roman soldiers, under
command of* AULUS.)

AULUS.

"Halt," men, and "Front !"   Now, Gavius, keep the
    ranks :
Nor roll away upon the grassy slope
Like a round mass of loosened stone.
(*Gavius had lounged on a couple of yards after
the command to halt.*)

GAVIUS (*aside, sneering*).

Too bad :
He drives us up and down with haughty tones,
As though he were a real corporal,

And not a private soldier in the ranks,
Of equal grade with us, but greater age ;
Who, chancing to be somewhat sooner born
(Through neither skill nor merit of his own),
Has consequently served a longer time
Than most of us who go along with him,
And so is placed in charge of the patrol.
Merely a jack-in-office !
  (*Gavius returns sulkily to his place in the ranks.*)

AULUS.

     Listen, men :
Our mission is accomplished : to observe
The cross-roads near this homestead, and to note
If there be any sign of marching troops,
Sent by our crafty Carthaginian foe,
To intercept our forces at the ford ;
There is no trace of any movement here.
So now the orders bid us start in haste,
To follow all our army in retreat.

GAVIUS (*sneeringly*).

Then may we, Aulus, ere returning home,
Since wines are generous here and women fair,
Provide ourselves with something suitable
Or pretty, as a present for our friends ?
    (*Speaking more earnestly.*)
We soldiers grumble not to leave the spoil,
To join in swift attacks and deadly strife ;
Yet, as we now march back to Italy,

(*Speaking with warmth.*)

Would it not be a pleasing thing·to take
Some charming dark-eyed Spanish maid ?　To show
How the Iberian sun can tinge the peach
With blushing bloom, and ripen ruddy fruit
Fit for the rosy god !

AULUS (*aside*).

Pernicious words :
Breathed by a ready reckless mutineer,
A cunning leader in the devil's cause,
Into young ears where they might fructify.
Now, after such a bid of bribery,
The men might disobey a plain command
To turn and leave the plunder offered them ;
I'll win their reason by good arguments,
And make a semblance of consulting them :
At least one vote is sure.

(*Aloud.*)

Soldiers, attend !
'Tis true were this some hostile foreign land—
Not friendly, neutral Spain, which still we hope
Some day to rescue from the Punic grasp—
Then custom would permit to take the spoil ;
But here we should refrain though holding power.
Our only duty is to gather news,
Not to disturb the peaceful Spaniard's home.
Further, I hold our honour and good name
In some sort pledged ; although we now retire
Beyond the reach of an avenging arm,

The peasants else might raise to punish us :
Guerilla warfare, profitless and dread.
I put it to the vote.   How say you, men,
That we should spare or take !

FIRST SOLDIER.

I say : "We spare."

SECOND SOLDIER.

I hold that Gavius has said well : "We take."

AULUS.

Then two wish either course ; so as the chief,
I must decide it by a casting vote :
"We spare."   And now let us away.

GAVIUS (*aside*).

A fraud !

(*Exeunt, marching.   Then enter from the house*
ALALIA *followed by* HERCTA ; *they prepare the
table under a tree for the repast,* HERCTA *bringing out dishes and plates, while* ALALIA *arranges
them.   Enter from the house* BASILIO.)

BASILIO (*peevishly*).

Already it is past the dinner hour,
To-day.

ALALIA.

Pray, father, to excuse us still,
Because Katharna has not yet returned
From meeting my Lord Hannibal at noon,
I trust, indeed, she will not be delayed ;
It gives me cause for serious doubt and dread
When she is absent in such troublesome times :
Though now the Roman troops have crossed the stream,
Apparently intent on marching north,
I hope peace is restored and she is safe.

BASILIO (*absently*).

A husband worthy of the purest blood
Of ancient Spain, which flows within our veins :
Though Fortune bids us live most frugally,
Nor dwell in castles suited to the rich.
And yet, Alalia, I tell you true :
All the high lineage of the Suffete's son,
With his great power and wealth, were naught to me,
Did I not know his suit is born of love,
And that Katharna's happiness depends
Upon their union, which may heaven bless !
But my old limbs already are fatigued,
So I will rest within until she comes.

(BASILIO *enters the house.*)

(*Enter* GAVIUS, *through some shrubbery, without
seeing* ALALIA *and* HERCTA.)

GAVIUS (*soliloquises*).

Hah, my good Aulus ! So you thought, indeed,
To have your way and trick me by the vote,
Rather than risk a downright mutiny. It seems
You failed to turn me from my fixed resolve ;
For if by chance some men decline their share
Of what the gracious gods bestow as spoil
Upon the toilers in a hard campaign,
The more remains for others, that is all.
Had you not picked a quarrel with me first,
For slouching, as you dared to term my gait,
I would have done your bidding readily ;
But that is past, and I am freed from you.
Which of us is most independent now ?
Alone, I guide my party at my will,
But you must join the host, and yield command
Of the small guard o'er which you lorded it.
Should I be guided by a pedant's wish ?
No. First I will enjoy each luxury,
Then find my own way back to Italy,
As military rules are so severe.

(*He sees* ALALIA, *who, observing the freedom of
his look and manner, shrinks back.*)

Ye gods ! I spoke prophetically, too :
Phrasing of ripened beauty's coloured cheek :
For, if the treacherous wine deceives me not,
Behold the dainty dame I dreamed about !

(*He reels slightly.*)

Yes, she shall be my lovely prize of war.

(*To* ALALIA.)

Come, dear, along with me to Rome !

ALALIA.

Help ! help !

(ALALIA *endeavours to escape.* GAVIUS *seizes and is dragging her away. she shrieks and faints.* BASILIO, *from the house, and* HERCTA, *rush forward to rescue her.* BASILIO *raises his stick in both hands to strike* GAVIUS *on the head.* GAVIUS *draws his sword and runs* BASILIO *through, killing him.* HERCTA *flies.* GAVIUS *bears away* ALALIA. *After a long pause, enter* KATHARNA.)

KATHARNA.

I bring good news for those who ever join
In sympathy with me.

(*She shrieks on seeing her father's body : at the same moment* HERCTA *runs out from behind the house.*)

My father ! Help !

O heaven ! Say, Hercta, what means this ?

(KATHARNA *hurries to her father : kneels beside him : examines his face, his eyes, and looks to see whether he breathes : feels his forehead, hand, and pulse at the wrist.*)

HERCTA.

Alas !

There came a Roman soldier flushed with wine,
And seized your sister who prepared the meal :

She struggled hard, shrieking aloud for aid ;
Your father quickly issued from the house
And strove to save her ; but the man, enraged,
Clutched at his sword and struck Basilio dead,
Then bore away Alalia in a swoon.
I fled in fear, but followed on the hill
Until I saw him wade across the ford ;
Then having safely gained the further bank,
He mingled with the crowd of baggage men
And motley followers.

KATHARNA.

Oh, alas the day !
My father dead : Alalia lost !   Then I——

(*She draws a dagger, raises it aloft, and is on the
point of killing herself : then lowers it.*)

Not so : fools plunge the weapons in their breasts,
The wise keep for their foes.

(*She replaces the dagger in her dress.   Still on her
knees she bends over her father's face.*)

I must be calm.
Speak to me, father, but a word again !
He moves !   Ah, no ; it was the spirit shade
Hovering an instant o'er its late abode !
Marking its presence by the quivering nerve,
As the soft zephyr touches tranquil pools,
Stirring the surface from its lifelessness.

(*She weeps.*)

How can I e'er repay you for your love,

Which dowered me with every happiness
That you could grant since I was yet a child ?
Yes, I was to be married soon, but now
Joy seems a treason to your memory.

(*She springs to her feet, and paces backwards and
forwards, with her hands clenched.*)

I vow to heaven to dedicate my life,
In filial duty, to obtain revenge :
Although it costs, as earthly sacrifice,
My dearest hopes, my love and happiness.
Immortal gods, behold my father's wrongs :
Record these solemn words, and grant me aid
To give them meaning !

(*She speaks hurriedly.*)

Hercta, I must go
Immediately !   But you shall stay behind
Until the coming of Lord Hannibal,
Who presently will seek me as arranged.
Tell him of the catastrophe, but say,
That as I followed to the river's brink,
Striving to save my sister from the fiend,
He turned and slew me : then the rushing waves
Swallowed me in their depths ; but as I fell
I called to you, "Tell Hannibal of this,"
And say I prayed him seek revenge for me.

(*She speaks deliberately.*)

Then having fired him thus, join me at once
Beside the temple ; bring sure-footed mules,
With saddle-bags containing simple food,
That we may fly beyond the reach of search.

(*She raises her voice.*)

So the balked lion in his agony
Will wreak on Rome dread vengeance for this deed !

(*Exit* KATHARNA.)

HERCTA.

Alas ! my master dead, under whose roof
I ever was retained with kindliness ;
Here I have passed a peaceful happy life,
Since left an orphan by the civil wars.
Of my dear mistresses yet one remains,
And so has greater claims upon my love,
Obedience, and devotion to her cause,
By which I might repay a trifling share
Of the great debt of endless gratitude
I owe herself and all her family.
Were it not better that Lord Hannibal
Should know the truth at once, and rescue her
From gloomy unprotected wanderings :
Meeting us at the fane, it would appear
As if kind fate had sent him to her aid !
It might be so, and yet no choice remains :
I must obey ; it is my only course
To follow out her wishes for the time ;
For it would be a cruel shame on me
To take her orders and betray the trust ;
But I will plead to her while not too late,
To turn her mind from all her misery,
Seeking her solace in a husband's love
And happiness.

(*Enter* HANNIBAL.)

HANNIBAL (*aside*).

Some evil fate is here !
(*Aloud.*)

What horror, Hercta !　Is Basilio dead,
Or merely swooning ?

HERCTA.

Dead, I fear, my lord ;
Alas ! if you had only chanced to come
Just one short hour ago, all had been well :
But now——
(*She weeps.*)

HANNIBAL.

How did this tragedy occur ?

HERCTA.

A Roman soldier, of a brutal mien,
Rushed from the wood and seized my mistress, first
Alalia, who cried aloud for help,
At which my master hurried to her aid ;
But the fierce Roman slew him with his sword,
And dragged his prize towards the river-bank.
My mistress, dear Katharna, then arrived,
And speeding after them most recklessly,
She overtook the robber at the ford ;
(*A pause.*)

Turning, he stabbed and hurled her in the stream !
(HERCTA *weeps.*)

HANNIBAL.

O heaven, help me !

HERCTA.

                    She was swept away,
Till, sinking, she called loud to me who watched,
To pray you be revenged for her on Rome !

                    (HERCTA *weeps.*)

HANNIBAL.

Ye gods ! there is no need to ask of me
To seek the vengeance fury bids me have !
From this hour forth I give my life to it.
To-morrow morning, as my father wished,
At Moloch's altar I will take the vow
That binds me to his service evermore !

                    (*He speaks hurriedly to* HERCTA.)

Now haste and lead me to the very spot
Near which you saw the lady disappear ;
For often currents cast upon the shores,
Or strand amid the shallows of the stream,
One fallen in the river far above ;
And if by chance this was the case with her,
We may not find her, even now, too late :
The spirit yet might be recalled to life ;
As chance stays but an instant and is gone
For ever from our grasp.   Haste, haste, lead on !

                    (*Exeunt.*)

SCENE V.

Before a Ruined Temple. Enter KATHARNA *and* HERCTA, *meeting.*

HERCTA.

Madam, the mules stand tethered at the gate,
With preparations, as you ordered me,
Completed.

KATHARNA.

Hercta, it is well, so far :
But I have waited long and anxiously
To learn the progress of the desperate plan
With which I charged you.

HERCTA.

Madam, it proceeds
By leaps and bounds.

(*Aside.*)

Indeed, I fear, too well !

(*Aloud.*)

Although you bade me do a painful deed,
E'en if necessity demanded it,
Yet I have done all you instructed me,
Within my power.

KATHARNA.

How did he bear the news?

HERCTA.

Lord Hannibal was seized by a fierce calm :
His mien was terrible, his words were few.

KATHARNA.

Alas ! So strong men suffer more than those
Who, weak in fibre, shriek and tear their hair.
What did he do and say ?

HERCTA.

My story heard,
He hurried to the river, searched the banks
For miles below, in hopes of finding you,
Cast by some friendly current on the shore :
Then, in despair, gave up the hopeless task ;
But, before leaving, he declared to me
That at the dawn to-morrow he would vow
Sealing his life to Moloch's services.

(*A pause.*)

He leads the army soon to Italy.

KATHARNA.

War is a hero's trade and suits him well ;
And yet, alas, that he should suffer thus :
He is so noble, kind, and generous !

HERCTA (*aside*).

Now is the moment ; I may rescue her !

(*Aloud.*)

I pray you, madam, pause while not too late
To end his cruel tortures and your own.
Permit me to return to him at once,
Saying that grief for your dear father's death
Had caused your flight, but you have now returned,
And wish to see him ere the sun be set.
As to the tale I told him—

(*A pause.*)

He shall think,
That, being anxious to conceal your flight,
I had invented it ; then, if enraged,
He seeks to punish me for trifling thus—
I'm swift and can elude him.

KATHARNA.

Hercta, no.
I am most grateful for your sympathy ;
But what you have proposed in kindliness
Cannot be carried out.   I must not change,
And will not even pause or hesitate.
I know full well, as your report has shown,
He loves me truly as I worship him :
That is a furnace fit to forge the blade !
Though misery must await both him and me,
Yet from the depth of all our suffering

Will rise, high-tempered, strong, a fiery sword,
Which he shall wield to be revenged on Rome.

> (*A pause, in the midst of which* KATHARNA *bursts
> into tears, and, covering her face with one hand,
> extends the other to* HERCTA, *who takes it.*)

Your plan's impossible, my dear : let's go.

> (*Exeunt.*)

SCENE VI.

*In front of the Carthaginian camp. The army formed
in order of battle ; in the centre is a stone altar,
decked with garlands of flowers. On the right of
the altar stands* HAMILCAR ; *and on his right the
staff are drawn up, including* GISCO, MAHARBAL,
and MUTHUMBAL, *holding a roll of papyrus and a
reed-pen, and having a black ink-bottle suspended to
the front of his girdle. In front of the altar stands*
MAGDASSAN. *At the back of the scene* HAMILCAR'S
escort and trumpeters form a line.

MAGDASSAN (*to* HAMILCAR).

My lord, it is a valued privilege,
Devolving upon me, to speak to-day
As second in command. I humbly bear,
From this great Carthaginian host arrayed,
To you its chief and Suffete, world-renowned :

Assurance of our earnest gratitude
For skilfully victorious guidance past,
Our firm devotion present and to come.
While we deplore the fulness of the years
Which hinders you from leading us again
When soon we start upon the road to Rome,
We are prepared to witness at this hour
The pious dedication of your son
Hasdrubal at the ever-sacred shrine
Of mighty Molock, here with honour raised,
To fight till Rome yields to him.   We receive
Obediently, with trust, the chief you give,
To guide us onward in the arduous strife.
Most earnestly we pray the fiery god
To bid him rise triumphant o'er his foes ;
That we may overcome all obstacles,
Gigantic difficulties, hardships, which
Beset the narrow frozen Alpine paths,
Over the dizzy heights amid the clouds,
Until at length we reach the fertile plains
Upon the distant sunny borderland
Of Italy.

HAMILCAR.

Magdassan, what could swell—
More than the choice of you as messenger,
A famous and a favoured general—
The honour which the army does to me,
In its kind homage to an aged chief,
Who ever prized the men as glorious sons ?
Express to them my deepest gratitude

For all their words of duty and of love.
They are the valiant troops whom Carthage thanks,
With glowing pride, for bravely-rescued Spain,
A brilliant jewel in her diadem,
And now to form a base from which to strike
A deadly blow against the flank of Rome.
But an old lion must at length repose,
And die at last of age, though spared by death,
Encountered long on hard-contested fields ;
Then must the lion's brood assume his place,
For which I dedicate a son to-day :
Would that it were my first-born, as the rite
Demands when offering to our chosen gods ;
But I have felt constrained to grant his prayer,
Bearing in mind his arduous services,
And named him ruler of Emporia
To serve an urgent matter of the heart,
Which binds with strongest bonds a warrior,
When honour and stern duty set him free.
For not less arduous is his chosen post :
And yet its nature will enable him
To sip the honey and cull the flowers
Of married bliss.

(HAMILCAR *makes a sign to* HASDRUBAL, *and
they draw nearer to the altar.*)

Bear witness, O ye gods !
That now in presence of this mighty host,
I dedicate to Moloch's services,
My son——

MUTHUMBAL (*aside*).

Who's this in haste approaching us?

(*Addressing* HAMILCAR.)

Hold, sir! Nor deem my conduct impious,
That I should interrupt the sacred rite!
See, yonder comes Lord Hannibal himself!

(*Aside.*)

Though scarce himself, I fear, to judge his look.

(*Enter* HANNIBAL, *pale and dishevelled.*)

HANNIBAL.

I, Hannibal, your eldest son, have come
To claim my destined vow in hate of Rome.
It was not fitting, when I thought to place
My selfish aims before the country's cause;
The august god, whose service I denied,
Reached forth his mighty arm and crushed my hopes.

(*He presses his hands to his face in anguish,
then recovers composure.*)

Pray ask no more.

(HASDRUBAL *makes way for* HANNIBAL
beside the altar.)

HASDRUBAL.

O Hannibal, you come
To conquer fate!

HAMILCAR.

Let it be so, my sons :
The gods decree in spite of human will !

(*A sunbeam falls on the ground before the altar.*)

MAGDASSAN.

Auspicious sign !   Look how the sun bursts forth,
Which hid till now his burnished face close-wrapped
Behind a sable cloak of thunder-clouds,
Embroidered with a fringe of golden light,
A token of the glory they concealed.

(*The sunbeam moves to the altar, envelops it,
and then remains stationary.*)

The ray moves to the altar !   See the light
Of Baal's countenance, which views our gift,
And smiles acceptance of the offering !

(*All present raise their hands towards the
altar in pious adoration.*)

(*Curtain.*)

ACT II.

SCENE I.

HANNIBAL'S *tent in front of the Carthaginian camp, on high ground overlooking the Trebia, which flows diagonally across the distant scenery ; beyond the river appears the Roman camp.* HANNIBAL *and* GISCO *are standing before the tent.*

HANNIBAL.

Gisco, now that a leisure hour has come,
Pray signal that the prisoners may attend,
And make my present orders known to them.
First, those who wish may freely join our ranks
To share the plundering of Italy.
The rest in single combat, man to man,
As chosen by the plan of casting lots,
May fight, if they should wish to try their fate.
To the brave warriors grant these worthy terms ;
The conquerors win both freedom and their arms,
The vanquished will be saved by certain death
From pining longer in captivity.
To this they will most readily agree ;
Then cry : " Ye soldiers of the Punic host,
As we are now invading Italy,

Your fate is what the prisoners gladly sought :
Death frees you if you fail, while if you win,
You gain life, triumphs, and more spoil than they ! "
So, Gisco, let stout combats such as these
Be fought before the camp of every column,
For bright examples.

GISCO.

Certainly, my lord,
It shall be done.

HANNIBAL.

Then since the Roman troops
Have reached the fords to-night, as if they wished
To cross the stream at dawn and seize the road
Of our retreat to Spain, by which we came :
Though we might now fall back and save the line
Which our position here must jeopardise,
Yet I would rather stand and tempt them on,
To crush them as they cross, or hurl them back
Into the seething flood to perish there ;
But if defeated, then our host is lost,
Having no refuge left to shelter in,
After abandoning all certain ways
By which we might escape in case of rout.
What leader ever tempted Providence
With rashness such as this ? For here it rests :
I hold, two armies striving in the field
Resemble swordsmen fighting on a plank
Which bridges an abyss between two cliffs :
For either force advances or retires,

But neither may remove to right or left,
Which I attempt by this manœuvring :
Yet I will ponder deeply over it.
Return, I pray you, long before the dawn,
And I will then decide anent this stroke
By which I win or lose.

GISCO.

I will, my lord.
(*Exit* GISCO.   *Enter a Carthaginian Officer.*)

OFFICER.

Most noble master, as our guards patrolled,
Searching a lonely track which leads from Spain,
They seized a straggler who was journeying thence—
A Roman soldier with a lovely dame
Whom he termed wife, though she denied the bond,
And craved the favour of an audience,
Saying you knew Alalia in Spain,
And that Katharna's sister now entreats
You may accord the boon.   .

HANNIBAL (*aside*).

Alalia found !
To what tumultuous thoughts her name gives rise.
(*To the Officer.*)
'Tis well ! conduct the lady here at once.
(*Exit Officer, who presently returns with* ALALIA ;
she throws herself at HANNIBAL'S *feet ; he takes
her hand and gently raises her.*)

ALALIA.

Save me, O save me, Hannibal, I pray,
From the degraded lot in which I live,
The drudge and mistress of a man I scorn,
Who beats me cruelly when in his cups—
The base deserter Gavius, who prefers
To plunder homesteads and oppress the weak,
Sooner than join his legion in the war ;
He killed my father and dishonoured me,
Tearing me from my happy peaceful home.

(ALALIA weeps.)

HANNIBAL.

Sister Alalia, remain in peace,
For you are safe from further cruel wrongs.

(To the Officer.)

Bring Gavius here in fetters.

OFFICER.

Yes, my lord.

(Exit Officer.)

HANNIBAL (hesitating).

I pray you to describe Katharna's fate,
Although to hear it may be terrible.

ALALIA (surprised).

The gods be praised, she was absent with you,
When we were crushed by fortune's heavy blow ;
It is not probable she came to harm.

HANNIBAL.

Thank heaven, but——

ALALIA.

Surely you have known of this?

HANNIBAL.

No, for I blindly trusted Hercta's word :
And yet her tale was false ; for it was this :—
She saw you seized, then poor Basilio killed,
And last, Katharna perished at the ford ;
For there she overtook your ravisher
In her bold efforts to recover you.

ALALIA.

No, 'twas not true, but as I said before.
Although I fainted when my father fell
And Gavius bore me off, my sense returned
Before we reached the ford to cross the stream ;
Indeed we were alone until we joined
The crowd of stragglers on the further bank,
Where many lingered after wading there,
Resting before they climbed the steep ascent
Above them.

HANNIBAL (*eagerly*).

Tell me where Katharna dwells :
For I will send a messenger to Spain,
With tidings of your rescue by my troops.

ALALIA.

Alas, I do not know her residence,
Since I was led away. I hoped indeed
You would have brought the welcome news to me
That she was safe.

HANNIBAL (*mournfully*).

Katharna disappeared :
I have not seen her since the tragedy—
Basilio's death and your captivity :
Nor have I gathered any news of her ;
And such accounts as Hercta rendered me,
Whatever be the cause, were not the truth,
As proved by your descriptions.

ALALIA.

Very strange !
For I have known and trusted Hercta long,
As one who always proved herself to be
Of sure veracity and faithfulness.
I can but deem it most improbable
That she should have misled you purposely,
Without some weighty motive, or the wish——

(*She pauses.*)

HANNIBAL (*quickly*).

Whose wish ? Katharna's ?

ALALIA (*after a pause*).

Yes.

HANNIBAL.

Then why ?

ALALIA.

Perhaps—
(*She pauses.*)

HANNIBAL.

I hold she should have trusted me at least,
Telling plain truth, and how her duty urged
For some delay, or bade her break with me,
And not have doomed me in my ignorance
To suffer endless misery.

ALALIA.

Perhaps
She could not trust herself, if you should plead
In the warm influence of an interview :
Having allies strong, numerous, subtle, bold,
Within her heart and mind to give you aid
Against the course that filial piety
Appeared to indicate.

HANNIBAL.

That may be so ;
She might have bidden Hercta tell the truth,
And yet have fled.

ALALIA.

You would have sought for her
With all your great resource and energy,
Rendering escape almost impossible ;
Once found, how could she have withstood your will ?
Surely her resolution would have failed.

(*Re-enter the Officer preceding* GAVIUS, *who is escorted
by a Carthaginian soldier, armed with a spear
in his hand and a dagger in his belt ; a Corporal
follows them, in command of the prisoner and
escort.* GAVIUS *is bare-headed and unarmed ;
his wrists are chained together in front of him.*)

HANNIBAL (*to* ALALIA).

Is this the man who scattered misery,
In wanton glee, midst innocence and peace ?

ALALIA.

Gavius it is, who has destroyed our house !

HANNIBAL (*to the Officer*).

Then let him die : away with him at once !

GAVIUS.

She has betrayed me : let her perish too !

(*In spite of his bound wrists,* GAVIUS *snatches the dagger from the belt of the Carthaginian soldier, and, making a rapid step forward, stabs* ALALIA, *who falls back into* HANNIBAL'S *arms.* GAVIUS *is seized by the Corporal and Soldier, disarmed, and dragged out for execution.*)

HANNIBAL (*to the Officer*).

Quick ! Bring a couch from yonder tent.

ALALIA.

I die ;
O Hannibal, it will be over soon,
And for the best.

(*The Officer draws forward a couch from the tent, and then follows* GAVIUS. HANNIBAL *allows* ALALIA *to sink down upon the couch, and then examines the wound.*)

HANNIBAL.

The coward left no hope.
I greatly grieve I did not caution you
In time to save you from approaching him.
Who would have thought, if not the fiend himself,
A prisoner guarded, bound, and quite unarmed,
Could strike the treacherous blow !

(*A pause.*)

Alalia, dear,
Now pausing on the threshold of the world,
Ere passing to the mystic land of shades,
With your prophetic vision clear and bright,
Say why Katharna hid her fate from me?

ALALIA.

Perhaps to guide you on to conquer Rome,
And so avenge her father's death and me ;
But (*a pause*) never doubt (*a pause*) Katharna's love for
    you.
So, when at last you meet her happily,
As much I hope you will, and all is well,
While a bright future shines before you both,
Then speak to her of poor Alalia's death,
And say affection bound me to the last
In the fond memory of our sisterhood.

(ALALIA *dies.*)
(*After a pause,* HANNIBAL *moves away a little, and beckons: re-enter the Officer, Corporal, and Soldier.*)

HANNIBAL.

Her gentle soul has fled : now bear her forth.
We'll bury her at dawn where violets bloom.

(*Exeunt the Officer, Corporal, and Soldier, carrying the couch on which lies the body of* ALALIA. *The light has gradually failed, and it now becomes dusk.*)

HANNIBAL (*soliloquises*).

See, the light fades, and kindly nature shrouds
The victim of a cruel tragedy.
Now I owe duty to my gallant troops,
My country, Carthage, and the fiery god :
So I must sleep if that be possible,
And gain new vigour for to-morrow's strife.
I will lie down at once within the tent,
Perhaps to rest, but how to sleep indeed,
When every chord of tender passion thrills,
Roused by Katharna's memory in my soul,
And sweet Alalia's death ?   But I must try.

(HANNIBAL *enters the tent and lies upon a couch,
within view, wrapped in a cloak. It becomes
dark :* HANNIBAL *sleeps and dreams. Enter a
vision of* KATHARNA, *pale and calm, and the
moonlight falls on her.*)

VISION OF KATHARNA.

O Hannibal ! I know your troubled thoughts :
Behold these signs and read.

(*The vision of* KATAHRNA *makes a wave of the
hand, and, as through a transparency, there
appears a town in ruins on one side, and the
forest cast down on the other , a gigantic serpent
moves between them with its head raised high in
the air, the remainder of its body being composed
of the long winding column formed by an army on
the march.*)

This scene portends
The devastation of fair Italy,
Which you shall soon achieve by force of arms :
Go boldly onwards ; never look again
Upon the road to Spain.

(*The allegorical view vanishes, and the vision of*
KATHARNA *partly fades.*)

Farewell ! Farewell !

(*The vision of* KATHARNA *disappears altogether :*
HANNIBAL *awakes, rises, and paces backwards
and forwards.*)

HANNIBAL (*anxiously*).

A dream which Moloch sent to me, perhaps,
To guide my course aright ; or else the trick
Of some fell demon luring on to doom.

(*A pause.*)

As to my life I am indifferent :
The heavens may threat to fall ; the tawny earth,
Opening its jaws, may menace to engulf,
Yet I remain unmoved and without dread ;
But for my country it is different,
Since her dear fate is given to my charge ;
And I must scan each move most cautiously,
However fair pretence may deck the lure.

(*A pause.*)

She promised I should conquer Italy :
A trap was never set without a bait ;

(*A pause.*)

And yet my judgment tells the plan is right :
No, no ; there is no fraud beneath the dream.

(Enter GISCO.)

GISCO.

My lord, I come according to command,
To learn your orders.

HANNIBAL.

Gisco, it is well :
In the dark, silent watches of the night
A vivid vision came to counsel me
To cast aside the rule of strategy,
That I might win the victory, as some
Left-handed swordsman disconcerts his foe,
However skilled he be ; for as I slept
I saw the very form and face of one,
A dear, lost friend, who promised victory ;
Bidding me not to heed the road to Spain ;
And see how truth shows further in her words :
For if, being vanquished, we attempt retreat,
The tribes behind would rise and bar our path,
Till, overtaken by the conquering foe,
We fall, surrounded by our enemies.
Choose either course, defeat is certain death,
And on that fact I base my reckoning :
The move is desperate, but the boldest best.
Then, Gisco, here we firmly hold our ground,
Abandoning the road that leads to Spain :
We tempt the Roman troops to cross the fords,
Then crush them in the act.

GISCO.

I understand :
The army will be glad to greet the news
That tells of coming conflict with the foe.

(*Exit* GISCO.)

HANNIBAL.

What puny trifles sometimes change our fate !
A Gavius lived, not even brave or true—
Vile, worthless, he had yet the power to mar
Katharna's life and mine, sending me here
Perhaps to overthrow his country's power,
When she might have escaped in whole or part.
Then see, the chain will drag another way :
Gavius bears off Alalia from her home ;
I meet her here, and view her tragic death,
And having spoken of her sister's fate,
Which fills my thoughts with her before I sleep,
I see my loved Katharna in a dream :
She solves the problem hatching in my brain,
Turning the scales which seemed so nicely poised
That I had almost chosen otherwise,
Instead of fixing on my present course.
Decisions such as this may shake the world :
Great in their failure, brilliant in success !
Which will it be ?   This dawning day will tell.

(*It becomes lighter.*)

But if this prove to be a warning dream,
Guiding me on to glorious victory,

Then I am chosen by the gods indeed
To extirpate the Romans and their sway !

(A pause.)

'Tis said in wine the mind perceives the truth :
So before battle when the nerves are strung.

(Exit.)

SCENE II.

Before HANNIBAL'S *tent on the field of Cannæ, after the battle : his third great victory, each of which resulted in the total destruction of a Roman army, the two previous victories being those of the Trebia and Thrasimene.   Enter* HANNIBAL, *accompanied by* GISCO, *and a Carthaginian Officer meeting them.*

OFFICER.

My lord, there have arrived from Capua,
Ambassadors seeking your powerful aid
Against the Romans.

HANNIBAL.

Pray admit them, sir.

(HANNIBAL *stands before the door of his tent.   Exit the Officer, who, presently returning, ushers in three Envoys, followed by Porters bearing presents of wine in amphoras, with flowers and fruit in gilded baskets.   The Envoys make obeisance before* HANNIBAL : *the Officer stands aside.*)

FIRST ENVOY.

Hail, mighty leader, who has crushed the power,
Till now invincible, of Roman arms !
We pray you to accept from Capua
These gifts in token of her fealty
And proffered services.

(*He motions to the Porters, who pass before* HANNIBAL
*exhibiting the contents of their jars and baskets
they then draw up at one side.*)

HANNIBAL.

I welcome you,
Ambassadors from " Capua the Fair ! "
And am most grateful for the gifts you bring,
With greetings to me in her honoured name.

(*At a sign from* HANNIBAL, *exeunt the Porters
conducted by the Officer.*)

FIRST ENVOY.

My lord, we viewed your progress hopefully,
Since first your conquering troops in triumph swept
Down on the fertile plains, as eagles swoop
From Alpine peaks.   Soon afterwards you hurled
The Roman legions into Trebia's stream :
Next drew Flaminius in the fatal snare,
Where calm Lake Thrasimene laves the strand :
There sank a Roman host to rise no more ;

And now a greater victory is won
By your small force against a giant foe,
Who thought to crush you in the river-loop,
Spread by the Aufidus behind your ranks ;
On Cannæ's field, the grave of Roman power,
Fell the third army of your enemies.
So does the hawk, with greater nerve and skill,
Defeat the cumbrous vulture's fierce attack,
And meet, by rapid moves, unwieldy strength.
This latest triumph may decide the war ;
Yet come what may command our city's aid ;
But strengthen us to ward the desperate strokes
Of Rome, whom we defy ; if still it be,
She has the will and power to turn on us
For vengeance.

HANNIBAL.

Sirs, I thank you from my heart,
For words so courteous and so flattering ;
I hope ere long to make your noble town
Unrivalled capital of Italy.
I gratefully accept the powerful help,
And should our foes assail your city walls,
My veterans shall assist your native force
To hurl them headlong from it.

SECOND ENVOY.

Nobly said,
By one whose deeds are weightier than words !
Now, gracious lord, we crave that you may deign,

On some auspicious day, to favour us
By a triumphant visit to our town,
When banquets, circus games, and festivals
Will mark the gladness of the citizens,
And their warm welcome to the honoured guest ;
While if you tarry through the winter months
We all will vie in hospitality,
Striving to make your gallant troops forget
The toils and hardships of their long campaigns.

HANNIBAL.

The honour will be mine, the pleasure ours,
Of coming as you courteously invite ;
Till then, my friends, farewell !

ENVOYS.

My lord, farewell !

(*Exeunt Envoys, conducted by* GISCO, *who then returns. Enter* MAHARBAL, *followed by* MAGO.)

HANNIBAL.

What news ?

MAHARBAL.

My lord, I hasten to report
The capture of the various Roman camps,
Where twenty thousand of their soldiers fled
After your victory of yesterday,
And now surrender, begging clemency.

But let the earliest fruits of victory
Not cloy your appetite for richer fare :
Upon the field of Cannæ we have found
A key which can unlock the gates of Rome !
Permit me to lead forward instantly
My bold victorious cavalry, who long
To light a bonfire on old Tiber's banks :
That all the nations may espy the flames,
And recognise the Carthaginian's hand !
The foe must see me first approach the walls
Before he hears that I am on the road ;
If you will follow with the infantry :
Then in four days at most, I promise you,
That we shall sup within the Capitol !

HANNIBAL.

Stay, good Maharbal : did success depend
Upon your valour, energy, and skill,
Or yet the prowess of your cavalry,
We should be sure to win the desperate game ;
But how could horsemen storm the battlements ?
They must await the coming infantry,
And thus surprise would fail ; nor does a siege
Afford much hope for half-disciplined troops,
Which scatter with their booty at their will :
To leave us weak, recoiling from the walls,
With foes to crush us ere we gather strength
To combat them anew ; then we should lose
The fruits of all our hard-gained victories ;
One such defeat would surely end our power :

Abandoned by allies, lacking a road
By which we could retreat, our fate were sealed.
But, Mago, hasten back to Carthage, now,
And clearly show the Senate all our needs ;
Entreat them to send me a powerful force
Of steady, seasoned, gallant Spanish troops :
Led by Hasdrubal, who, I am advised,
Having restored peace to Emporia,
Has now been summoned to command in Spain,
Upon our venerable father's death,
Of which the sad news came but yesterday,
And will await the word to join us here.
On the arrival of such powerful aid,
We should be equal to the siege of Rome ;
Nor need we quit her till she falls to us ;
If not, her life would mean our country's death.

MAGO.

Brother, my mission shall be as you wish ;
I go at once.

(*Exeunt all but* HANNIBAL.)

HANNIBAL.

Another victory !
Such triumphs overleap my highest hopes ;
Great is the promised vengeance I have wreaked
In the fierce battles of these long campaigns ;
Offering by death whole hosts of warriors,
From the accursed race I swore to hate,

As sacrifices to my diety.
Haste ! Haste, the fated day if vanquished Rome
Is doomed to perish by great Moloch's will !

(*Exit.*)

SCENE III.

*Grove of the temple of Ashtaroth, the moon-goddess, at
Carthage. Enter* MUTHUMBAL *and* HERCTA, *meeting.*

MUTHUMBAL.

Why, Hercta !

(HERCTA *hurries forward, and extends both hands,
which* MUTHUMBAL *grasps.*)

HERCTA.

You, Muthumbal !

MUTHUMBAL.

Yes, indeed :
\What heavenly power has sent you ?

HERCTA.

It is fate,
Which gladdens me as well, by bringing here
A friend to greet me amongst foreigners.

MUTHUMBAL.

What tempted you to Carthage ?

HERCTA.

By mere chance,
I travelled with a wealthy dame from Spain,
Camilla is her name, who settled here
Not long ago.

MUTHUMBAL.

Thank goodness you have come ;
May we meet often, is Muthumbal's prayer.

HERCTA.

If you still care, I'll do so willingly.

MUTHUMBAL.

Care, Hercta ?
HERCTA (*pouting*).

Well, 'tis long since last we met
And passed so many pleasant hours in Spain.

MUTHUMBAL.

If this were not a public place, my dear,
Where grave men's eyes would mark a levity,
And sombre minds might deeply censure me,
Then I would offer you a gentle sign

That my affection lasts for ever true.
I long to add fresh memories to the old,
Of happy days that I have spent with you ;
Nor do I care for pleasing novelty,
Which might have tempted men more frivolous
To waver in your absence, and forget
The fading forms of charming scenes long past.

HERCTA.

Tell me, Muthumbal, how you prosper here ?

MUTHUMBAL (*looking proudly around*).

No more a warrior in the Punic host,
Where, I may mention confidentially,
I aided much the difficult success
And glorious triumph of our arms in Spain !
I am the trusted scribe of Malchus now,
Able lieutenant of our governor,
The Suffete Hanno, whose wise policy
Controls our state with undisputed sway,
Since great Hamilcar's recent death in Spain,
And while bold Hannibal remains abroad ;
But often when the Suffete is oppressed
By difficult matters and cares of state,
He will consult with Malchus, who asks me
To prompt his ready judgment of the case !

(*Proudly.*)

'Tis then some happy stroke of genius shines,
In Punic policy, to light the world :

And all men marvel at its brilliancy,
Giving the glory to the Suffete's skill,

(*Mournfully.*)

While its true author is Muthumbal, here :

(*Dismally.*)

Doomed like a root to lie beneath the ground,

(*Jauntily.*)

But able to force up the vigorous stem
Which bears sweet flowers and fruit to bless mankind !

HERCTA.

Is Malchus a good master to you now ?

MUTHUMBAL (*after a pause*).

He's kindly.

HERCTA.

How : not kind without being good ?

MUTHUMBAL.

He gives me little rank and smaller pay ;

(*A pause.*)

Yet once he saved my life.

HERCTA (*clasping her hands*).

Oh, how was that ?

MUTHUMBAL.

One day when he was acting on my hint,
A weighty business failed ; had he but told,
In explanation, that the plan was mine,
The raging Hanno would have had me slain
To ease his bile !

HERCTA.

But Malchus did not tell?

MUTHUMBAL.

Good Malchus kept his counsel, and I live !

HERCTA.

To give no credit when you guide them right,
Yet kill you if your best advice prove wrong,
Is neither justice nor humanity.

MUTHUMBAL (*bitterly*).

And yet it is a worldly way, I fear :
The strong to seize upon the better prize,
And cast the burdens on the helpless crew
Whose backs must bear them.

HERCTA (*persuasively*).

Come, Muthumbal, come
You are embittered by your grievances,
And take a much too gloomy view of life ;

Ungenerous to the wise, the kind, and just,
To those who freely give a liberal share
Of wealth to aid the cause of charity,
And find their happiness in doing good ;
As well as those who, having lions' strength,
Hold back their powers in noble equity,
Supporting what is right and for the best.
Consider this, and do not yet despair
Of human nature.

(*A pause.*)
      Malchus took the blame :
Did Hanno threaten him with death ?

MUTHUMBAL.

        Oh, no :
He could not spare him.   There are many scribes,
So in my case it would be different.

(*A pause.*)
'Twas no mean danger that Malchus incurred,
Braving the open or the secret force
Of Hanno's wrath, to shield a humble scribe.
His kindness touched me, for he took the blame.

HERCTA.

Did Hanno punish him in lesser ways ?

MUTHUMBAL.

Not so, for Malchus might have sought revenge,
Using for mischief any casual power,

Given by the knowledge of his master's plans,
Or the dark workings of his policy ;
Deep secrets which are hidden from even me,
And might not bear inspection.

HERCTA.

            To live thus,
When any day your work might earn the cross,
Is terrible !

MUTHUMBAL.

        Indeed, it would be so ;
But since luck saved me and my life escaped,
Through my good master's kindly clemency,
Having in view to run no second risk,
I have adopted a more prudent course,
Persuading Malchus, with some share of skill,
The thoughts I suggest are his own ideas ;
Thus he accepts the bantlings readily,
And fathers them in triumph or defeat.

HERCTA (*dubiously*).

The plan succeeds, then ?

MUTHUMBAL.

            Yes, it does, my dear

HERCTA (*laughing*).

Well done, Muthumbal ! Your are wise enough,
And may be trusted to protect yourself.

But I must hasten to my mistress now :
So, fare-you-well !

MUTHUMBAL.

Say, will you meet me here,
At the same hour to-morrow evening ?

> (HERCTA *runs backwards, smiling and kissing
> the tips of her fingers to him.*)

HERCTA.

Aye, if all's well !

MUTHUMBAL.

Good-bye, my love, till then !

> (*Exeunt.*)

SCENE IV.

*A street in Carthage, outside the Senate-House. Enter the
Suffete* HANNO *in a state litter, escorted by soldiers,
and attended by* MALCHUS. HANNO *alights from the
litter, and turns to the bearers and escort.*

HANNO.

Wait for me over there a little while.

> (*They obey.*)

Now, Malchus, we approach the Senate-House,

So I must choose quickly the wisest course ;
For I can never make my will prevail
Without clear definitions of my wish,
Born of a settled plan.   I think it best
To grant at once the force that Hannibal
Asks through his brother Mago at our hands ;
What other answer could we send to him,
Supported by the people ?

MALCHUS.

Good, my lord,
You surely would not thus decide in haste
To send the troops, if I could clearly show
That course is fraught with danger to the State ?
Suppose that Hannibal should conquer Rome,
Who would be master of the Punic world ?
Where would be then your present dignity
As ruler, with a beneficent sway ?

(*Aside.*)

The need of my advice, or the full power
To fittingly reward me for the aid !

(*Aloud.*)

Great Hannibal, the irresponsible,
Would crush resistance to his sovereign will ;
Who could deem that an end to be desired,
For freedom's cause or yet our country's good ?
Not I, for one, sir !

HANNO.

Weighty reasons, friend :
And as our nation's interests are at stake,

'Tis better not to grant the Spanish troops ;
But would the populace approve ?

MALCHUS.

No doubt :
I thought of that matter when coming here ;
And hold you may divert the people's thoughts
From Hannibal remaining without help ;
For they will thank you for a holiday,
Nor pay new taxes for a distant war.
Declare in open Senate that to aid
Our righteous cause of arms throughout the world,
'Tis best to pray to the immortal gods,
And name a day for human sacrifice
At Moloch's shrine.   The priests will praise your plan,
Strengthening your power with all their influence ;
They long have sought an opportunity
To punish sinners who despise the gods,
Holding the flamens as of little worth ;
For which offences they would levy fines,
Or seize the children of such impious men
As a fit sacrifice for Moloch's fire :
And might it not be useful to my Lord,
In contumacious cases of dissent,
From your benign, enlightened policy,
If you could cause a hint to be conveyed,
That if the parents' conduct should accord
More with the obvious wishes of the gods—
Which are, of course, interpreted by you—
To give support to all your arguments,

Their children might be safer from the flames?
Think what a mighty stimulus is here
To flagging zeal, and what a straightener-out
Of crooked consciences!

HANNO.

All very true:
It shall be managed as you have proposed.

(HANNO *enters the Senate-House*
Exit MALCHUS.)

SCENE V.

Reception-room in the mansion of KATHARNA, *at Carthage*
where she is now dwelling under the name of CAMILLA
KATHARNA *seated, engaged with crochet-work i,*
coloured worsteds.   Enter a Slave.

SLAVE.

Madam, the Suffete Hanno has arrived:
Waiting your gracious pleasure, he requests
The favour of an interview.

KATHARNA.

Indeed?
Admit his Excellency.

(*Exit Slave, who presently returns conducting* HANNO, *and then withdraws.* KATHARNA *rises, smiling, and bows to* HANNO; *then motions him to be seated, and resumes her seat.*)

KATHARNA.

Good, my lord,
What lucky chance has turned your busy thoughts
From stern affairs of state to me?

HANNO.

I pray,
Fair lady, tell me first: why does the flower,
After night's darkness, turn towards the sun
And watch, entranced, his course—imbibing life?
For then I will explain the simile.

(*A pause.*)

As the bright sun eclipses moon and stars,
So do you ever shine pre-eminent
Amongst the Punic dames; by every right
Of beauty, charm, and worth.

(HANNO *bows.*)

KATHARNA.

But surely, sir,
No cloud obscures the Punic firmament;
The rising fortunes of your mighty state
Are most auspicious, since proud Rome lies crushed
Beneath the deadly blow of Cannæ!

HANNO (*drily*).

Yes ;

May they remain so is my prayer, and yet
I fear they will not always triumph thus,
In warfare carried on beyond the seas ;

(*A pause.*)

Although a public holiday is fixed,
For human sacrifice at Moloch's shrine,
To pray him aid our forces.

KATHARNA.

Is that all,
When Mago has arrived to ask for help,
To reap the harvest ready for the blade ?

HANNO.

'Tis true, but neither can we spare the cost,
On account of our heavy taxes here ;
Nor yet Hasdrubal from the strife in Spain,
Where his brave troops still carry on the war
With the last army sent by sea from Rome
Against him.

KATHARNA.

Surely you will not rely
Entirely, noble Suffete, on your prayers ;
For would the gods believe you are sincere ?
Now send Hasdrubal and his force from Spain,
As Hannibal entreats, who knows the need ;
Do this in place of human sacrifice.

HANNO (*dubiously*).

Madam, the matter seems to move you much.

KATHARNA.

It does, my lord, because of gratitude
For Carthaginian hospitality ;
And also that I have inherited
A deadly feud with Rome ; then know besides,
I am a native of a distant land,
Where we believe that human sacrifice
Is only grateful to the gods above
When offered boldly on the battle-field,
In open warfare.

HANNO.

'Twould be difficult
To alter now the well-considered plans,
Approved already by the Senators
At my suggestion.

KATHARNA.

Difficult to some :
Not to my lord, whose lightest wish is law.

HANNO (*smiling*).

I would, dear madam, it were so with you !

KATHARNA (*coyly*).

Why ?

HANNO (*passionately.*)

Inspired by my ardent love,
I'd dare to claim the fruits———

KATHARNA (*averting her face*).

The fruits of love?
(*A pause, during which she appears to hesitate ,
she then continues with downcast eyes.*)
Who knows what conquests you may not achieve
If you will send the force?
(*A pause, after which she raises her eyes,
and meets his gaze.*)
Yet no true knight
Barters brave deeds against a lady's smiles,
But strikes a gallant blow in hopes of them,
Founding his claim for the desired rewards
Upon her gratitude.

HANNO (*aside*).

I'll hazard it !
(*Aloud and eagerly.*)
It shall be as you wish ; the troops shall go
Upon the mystic plea that I have seen
Great Moloch, who appeared and ordered me
To send Hasdrubal on to Italy,
And sacrifice in battle Roman hosts
Instead of children at his Punic shrine.
But when it is resolved upon, I trust
We meet?

KATHARNA (*with charming embarrassment*).

Say rather, when the force arrives
At its due destination ; then command
Camilla, who meanwhile must bid adieu.

(*She rises smiling, and bows to* HANNO,
who smiles and bows.)

HANNO.

Madam, I then remain your slave, as now.

(*Exit* HANNO.)

KATHARNA.

I trust the desperate game I play is won,
And Hannibal will gain the wished-for aid.
I dwell in Carthage but to serve the cause :
For this I lead the odious Suffete on,
And bandy triflings hurtful to my fame ;
For vengeance now I stake my life ; and yet
I guard intact my honour, come what may.

(*Exit* KATHARNA.)

ACT III.

Scene I.

Entrance to the temple of Jupiter at Rome. Within it can be seen a crowd, many of whom are women, leading or carrying children. The people are bowing and bending the knee, or kneeling and lying prostrate on the ground ; occasionally rising and extending their arms towards the statue of Jupiter, which stands at the further end of the temple. The women have dishevelled hair, and the whole appearance of the people suggests terror and distress. Enter Scipio.

Scipio.

Wild panic and confusion everywhere :
The weak turn traitors and the strong turn weak ;
Thus paralysed by Hannibal's approach,
We might conclude an ignominious peace,
Opening the gates to Punic treachery,
And choosing a short road to meet our doom ;
But I must thwart this fatal policy ;
So I have bribed the cunning soothsayers,
To find the mystic omens favourable
For stout resistance and continued war,

Promising that our triumph is secure
If we will persevere courageously.

(A pause.)

My will must rule the Senate and the town :
Why have they made me Consul otherwise ?
Besides, they owe me all their gratitude,
For I regained our Spanish provinces
After Hasdrubal marched for Italy ;
Though having quickly come by sea to Rome,
I'm here before he can arrive by land ;
So if Rome will but act obediently,
I'll guide her right, and save our fortunes yet.

> (<i>Enter two Senators meeting in the street : and on the
> steps of the temple, the high priest of Jupiter,
> from within.</i>)

FIRST SENATOR (excitedly).

Rome's fate is sealed, unless we come to terms
With this barbarian horde and conquering chief ;
We'll send ambassadors to sue for peace
At once !

SECOND SENATOR (gloomily).

      The city walls will check their course
Until we barter all we have for peace !
But never can we conquer in a siege
A man who always triumphs.

SCIPIO.

      Hold, my friends :
Indeed I trust that you exaggerate

Our danger and the helplessness of Rome ;
For when the struggle's in the open field,
Then armies seem to me like earthen jars,
Which floating down a stream collide with force
While fate sinks one, perhaps the other swims ;
But what can save the bowl, borne on the waves
Of some wild flooded river, 'gainst the rocks ?
Then let us welcome Hannibal's attack,
If fate should drive him on to dash his strength
Against walls which hot hatred cannot melt ;
Nor could the Carthaginian's fiery mood
Consume these faithful blocks of patient stone !
Moreover, by the grace of Jupiter,
A day shall come when through a great defeat,
Or else exhaustion from protracted war,
The Punic power will fail in Italy ;
Then shall arrive a time when we may pen
The Carthaginian wolf within his lair,
And drive him forth to die upon our spears !
But now let every Roman's heart be firm ;
Do not beg mercy from a cruel foe,
Who only deals in Punic treachery.
The mighty power and dignity of Rome
Rest on her gallant offspring's fortitude ;
And shall *we* be the first to seal their doom ?
Think that our honour is in jeopardy !

FIRST SENATOR.

My lord, your judgment is experienced
Through *long* and arduous service in the field ;

So if you deem resistance for the best,
As not without the hope of victory,
What can we say who speak by theory?
Your skilled advice must guide us.

SECOND SENATOR.

'Tis well said ;
I do not understand the use of walls,
But thought them built for foes to batter down,
Instead of, as you have explained to us,
To lure bold rams to crush their butting heads.

HIGH PRIEST.

Well spoken, noble Consul Scipio !
Accept the leadership, for you are skilled
In council and the conduct of a war.
Even from flames and ashes Rome would rise,
Like the young phœnix, and renew the fight.

(*He raises his voice, and addresses the crowd
now issuing from the temple.*)

Have courage, citizens, and shun despair ;
For the immortal gods will strengthen us
To wreak a signal vengeance on our foes,
Who worship Baal with human sacrifice !

FIRST CITIZEN.

Our courage shall not fail !

OTHER CITIZENS.

Never till death !

HIGH PRIEST.

'Tis well, my sons.   Now let your firm resolve
Inspire your friends with equal fortitude.
Say Scipio demands that Rome stands firm :
And the High Priest of Jupiter proclaims
That the great gods will aid us !

CITIZENS.

Yes, } We will !
Aye. }

(*Exeunt.*)

SCENE II.

Before the Colline Gate, Rome.   Enter HANNIBAL
*attended by officers ; also to the right and left Car-
thaginian archers and slingers.   They approach the
gate.*

HANNIBAL.

Well done, good marksmen ; you have cleared the wall !
There's not a crop-haired Roman to be seen,
And now it seems to hedge an empty town ;
Yet, close behind those massive beams of oak,

There lurks the foe prepared for devilment,
Like the fierce badger in his narrow hole.
Although they cannot see me, yet they hear
What I proclaim aloud before these doors,
That I will soon redeem my vow of hate
After Hasdrubal's army has arrived,
Which, 'tis well known, is now upon the way
To reinforce my power and join the siege ;
But in the meanwhile there are Latin towns
Unfortified and lying helplessly,
Which owe allegiance to hard-stricken Rome,
And now shall pay for it by servitude ;
There we will wait the coming of our troops.

> (*Exeunt. As they retire, Roman soldiers appear upon the walls, yelling after them and brandishing weapons.*)

SCENE III.

Before HANNIBAL'S *tent in the Carthaginian camp near Rome. Enter* HANNIBAL *attended by* GISCO *and* MAGO.

HANNIBAL.

Ere now Hasdrubal's army, probably,
Has approached northern Italy.   At least
We know the date on which his force set out ;
And reckoning for a march so arduous,
He should be nearing soon our battle-fields

Or theatre of war.   'Tis very strange
No speedy messenger has arrived yet,
To tell his progress, and concert with me
How we could best combine to crush the foe.
Has Consul Claudius Nero checked his march?
If so, I pray it may not be for long;
But stranger, Mago, is what you relate,
That Hanno's influence procured this help
Which I sought from the Senate.

MAGO.

                        Yes, most strange,
After he had opposed it bitterly;
He changed, and led with him the Senators
To give approval to the scheme you wished.

HANNIBAL.

'Tis marvellous!   Perhaps in the cold breasts
Of those who hunger but for gaudy power,
And gain their selfish ends by truckling
To ignorance and narrow prejudice,
There lurks a secret spark of patriotism,
Which being fanned by chance enflames the soul,
Firing to noble deeds.
                                        (*A pause.*)
                    But who comes here?
There's something wrong, to judge his troubled face,
His dull and downcast mien.
                    (*Enter a Carthaginian Officer.*)
                    What tidings, sir?

OFFICER (*gloomily*).

I hastened from the outposts here, my lord,
And bring grave news, if true.
(*He opens a cloak which he is carrying, and discloses
a human head, with a sheet of papyrus attached
to the hair.*)
Soon after dawn
A Roman cast this head before our lines,
With gestures to invite our noticing ;
Then, seeing that our sentries had observed,
And some were moving to the spot, he fled.
I'll wait without, my lord, in case of need
For further questioning.
(*Exit Officer.* HANNIBAL, *who has taken the head,
holding it partly wrapped in the cloak, reads an
inscription on the papyrus.*)

HANNIBAL (*reading*).

" Hasdrubal's head,
Which Claudius Nero sends to Hannibal."

MAGO.

Hasdrubal dead !

HANNIBAL.

I mourn my brother's death,
And see before me here my country's doom.
Hasdrubal's army has been overthrown,
And Carthage will decline to send more aid.

Now Rome will be indeed impregnable,
And soon will seek revenge on Punic soil,
Remembering that our peaceful citizens
Are busy traders, quite unused to arms.
They dread a siege by Rome, and yet withhold
The full supplies to wage a distant war,
Which might have saved them.   Here behold a sign,
A head, the symbol of a nation's death !
Gisco, I would be some brief space alone,
To ponder on my brother's memory ;
But, Mago, first let us converse of it.

GISCO.

Peace be with you and bold Hasdrubal's manes !

(*Exit* GISCO.)

MAGO.

There never beat a stouter heart than his,
Or one more kind and true.

HANNIBAL.

He died for us.

(*Exeunt.*)

SCENE IV.

Reception-room in KATHARNA'S *mansion in Carthage.*
Enter KATHARNA, *and presently a Slave.*

SLAVE.

Madam, the Suffete Hanno has arrived,
And seeks the favour of an interview.

KATHARNA.

Admit his worship.

(*Exit Slave.*)

KATHARNA (*raising her hands towards heaven*).

Ye immortal gods,
Assist me in this crisis !

(*Enter* HANNO.)

KATHARNA (*bowing*).

Good, my lord,
You are most welcome in my humble home.

HANNO (*bowing low*).

Madam, I come by your permission given
At our last meeting, which seems years ago ;

Borne on the wings of love, I spurn the ground,
And count the very winds of heaven too slow
To bear me in my eager flight to you !

KATHARNA.

My lord, you have already truly won
Camilla's gratitude ; nobler by far,
You wisely strove to serve your country's cause,
Although we must deplore a great defeat ;
Hasdrubal's army failed, doomed and destroyed,
Nor reached its goal of joining with the host
Of Hannibal ; to whom, I pray, despatch
A stronger force to gain complete success,
And win for you the favours, which mischance
Still leaves somewhat beyond your certain reach
For their attainment.

> (KATHARNA *partly bows to* HANNO, *partly lowers
> her face and eyes ;* HANNO *starts, then after a
> pause replies.*)

HANNO (*impatiently*).

Madam, now in truth,
I would convey the glancing sunbeams here
To give you joy, but the stern fates forbid.
Indeed, you wish a thing impossible,
Since Carthage will not grant more troops for this ;
While even now the disappointed mob,

Which yesterday applauded, seeks my blood,
Crying, I sent Hasdrubal to his doom.

(*Earnestly.*)

I pray, then, grant the longed-for priceless boon
You promised me?

(*A pause, after which* HANNO *continues,
warmly and proudly.*)

              Command me if you will,
Proving devotion and my ardent love,
To strive to reach far Eziongeber,
By rounding the South Horn and outstretched arm
Of Aromata! Bid me sail four moons
To westward of the land, through waves and clouds,
Where ocean grasses rope-like bind the prows
Amid the roar of distant cataracts,
While blood-red fogs obscure the setting sun,
And mystic breezes laden with perfume
Soothe all the crews to sleep, so that their minds,
Bewitched, can ne'er recall their voyages!

(*A pause, during which* KATHARNA
does not respond.)

Or fly with me to that bright halcyon isle,
Of late discovered, and which lies midway
Upon the heaving bosom of the deep,
Where golden sands are laved by silvery seas,
And mountains rise on mountains, peaks on peaks,
Until the highest granite spire attains

(*He raises his hand above his head and
points upwards.*)

To realms beyond the ken of mortal man ;
While on the summit of the pinnacle
The heavens are fixed, and round it stars revolve.

(He lowers his hand.)

To mirror nature limpid rivers flow,
Where, clothed in ever-verdant garb, there dwells
Perennial Spring on forest, field, and flood.
You shall be queen of that fair paradise,
There tranquilly to dwell in sylvan peace,
Or, like a second Dido, found a world !
Consorting with you I will there renounce
The pomps and power, the strife of government,
For evermore, which here engross my life.

(A pause.)

KATHARNA.

My lord, I thank you, but I crave your grace,
I have already answered.

HANNO (indignantly).

Pause, reflect ;
For, madam, it is scarcely suitable
I should be lightly spurned, as though I were
Some simpering garland-ornamented youth
Who fails to please, but ever dances on
Before you in faint hope !

(HANNO pauses ; KATHARNA is silent ; and HANNO
continues, becoming calmer.)

                    For still the power,
Which at your bidding sent Hasdrubal forth,
Is strong in Carthage, and can work my will
If fair persuasion fails.   Camilla, say,
Have you no kinder word before I go ?

KATHARNA.

Alas, no other, sir ; I spoke my mind.

HANNO (*enraged*).

Then heaven help you when you pray for aid !

                              (*Exit* HANNO.)

KATHARNA (*after a pause*).

I almost answered with another threat,
When he was raving of his mighty power ;
But I have greatly angered him, 'tis true,
And duped him thoroughly to gain my ends,
So that he may, by right, complain of me.
Since Hannibal was far and I alone,
I worked with ready wit and smiling mien ;
At first they triumphed, now I fear they fail !

                                   (*Exit.*)

SCENE V.

The Grove of the Temple of Ashtaroth, at Carthage.
Enter MUTHUMBAL : *he examines a sun-dial.*

MUTHUMBAL (*gloomily*).

Preserve us, heaven !   'Tis past the promised hour,
By several notches on the tell-tale dial,
Yet Hercta is not here : she may not come.
Ah, what a painful thought, to be in doubt
As to the cause, perhaps for many hours !

(*Pensively.*)

To-morrow is uncertain, for this night,
As Hanno bids, her mistress will be seized :
For Hercta's safety there's anxiety ;
But dare I warn her ?   No, for she might tell
Her mistress, whom she loves so faithfully ;
And did Camilla learn the threatened blow
Impends above her head, she would escape ;
But Hercta will be rescued by her wit,
And if no roof protects her in her need,
To pass one night beneath the brilliant moon,
On soft and verdant Carthaginian lawns,
Amidst the beauteous flowering shrublets' shade,
Breathing soft air, heavy with sweet perfumes,
Would be no hardship ; and the friendly night
Can hide with sable cloaks her loveliness,
Which otherwise might tempt some loiterer
To jeopardise her honour and my love ;

So I must meet and guard her at the dawn,
To part no more from her : leading her home,
Where, as my wife, she will be quite secure.

(Gloomily.)

But why delays my fair one, dallying thus ?
Perhaps she has begun to cool to me !

(Reflectively.)

Yet, patience ; wait and see ; don't fear the worst !

(Satirically.)

A woman must attire herself, to add
New lustre to her charms ; forgets the hour,
Or, noting it, delays, knowing full well
Poor old Muthumbal still must wait for her !

(Quickly.)

There's some one passing through those shrubberies ;

(Joyfully.)

Great Tanit bless her : now she comes at last !
Away with doubts ; away with carking care ;
Nor scare my darling with a gloomy face
When greeting her !

(Enter HERCTA, *smiling.)*

HERCTA.

                    Muthumbal, pray forgive
The great delay ; my mistress kept me long ;

(Coquettishly.)

Stern duty often bars a pleasant road—
Sometimes for ever.

MUTHUMBAL.

Now, all's well : you're here
Indeed, you were forgiven before you asked ;
And yet I wish a favour in return :
'Tis that we meet to-morrow at the dawn,
Instead of at the hour the fiery god
Falls in the western ocean.

HERCTA.

I will try ;
But why, Muthumbal, do you name the dawn?
My mistress often needs my services
So early.

MUTHUMBAL.

Well, my love, 'tis for your good ;
But promise me to come, if you are free
To carry out your pledge.

HERCTA.

And why not free ?
Speak, good Muthumbal, speak.   I pray you trust
Your Hercta, and explain the mystic plot
That lies between your sayings and your mind ;
For if indeed you cannot yet rely
On the discretion of your lover's will,
As trust brings trust, the want of it, the want :
Then how can I, a helpless woman, rest
With confidence upon your guarding arm ?

And if you will not make a sacrifice,
But must refuse a boon to her you love,
Consider well what bitter seed you sow,
For I must surely know the truth at last
Which you hold back from me !

MUTHUMBAL (*reluctantly*).

Let it be so ;
But pledge your word to guard as secret news
All that I tell, and ne'er to be divulged.

HERCTA.

I promise you.

MUTHUMBAL (*earnestly*).

Then listen to my tale.
This night the mob—raging at our defeat,
Spying out treason in Camilla's mind,
And that she used a secret magic spell,
By which she urged the wavering Suffete on
To send Hasdrubal's force—will seize on her
And bear her captive, waiting Hanno's will.
'Twas Malchus who designed this treachery
At Hanno's wish, and roused the populace.
Though vainly, I endeavoured to dissuade
Ere Malchus broached the matter to his lord ;
And after, 'twas too late. So Hercta, dear,
Avoid the danger by an early flight ;
Meet me at break of day, and until then,
Heaven guard you safe from harm !

HERCTA (*aside*).

I must away
And warn my mistress.

(*Aloud.*)
Love, your heart is good :
I thank you for the news, and I will come.

(*Exeunt.*)

SCENE VI.

Reception-room in KATHARNA'S *mansion in Carthage.*
KATHARNA *seated, engaged in crochet-work. Enter*
HERCTA *hurriedly.*

HERCTA.

Fly, madam, fly ; for even now the mob,
Raging with fury, comes to seize on you !
Muthumbal, whom I knew of old in Spain,
Is now the scribe of Malchus, and lives here :
He told me, being anxious for my life,
And bade me to escape.   Malchus has raised
The wanton crowd, and cried you had bewitched
The Suffete's mind with charms of sorcery,
Till Hanno, yielding, sent Hasdrubal on
To perish with his host.   Thus I have gained
The warning from Muthumbal just in time ;
His death were sure, if his fierce master knew
He had betrayed the secret thus to me
Which rescues you !

KATHARNA.

True friend, indeed I owe
My life and honour to your faithfulness !
Quick ! Fetch me here a peasant's shawl and gown,
That I may pass unnoticed through the gates.
                    (*A confused sound of distant voices is heard,*
                                    which grows louder.)
Already I can hear the rabble's shouts
Outside !

HERCTA.

I'll bring the dress.
(*Exit* HERCTA. *Further clamour is heard, louder*
than before. *Enter* MALCHUS, *accompanied by*
MUTHUMBAL *and* ABDALONIM, *and followed*
by a mob armed with sticks, swords, bows, and
spears.)

KATHARNA (*indignantly*).

                              Explain this force !
What means your sudden advent ? Are you sent,
Or come of your own will ? Disclose your names.

MALCHUS.

Pardon us now ; we are to lead you hence,
To Suffete Hanno, unto whom complaint
Is made by many tongues, the breath of fame :
That you conspired against our Commonwealth.
Pray, know that Malchus is my humble name.

KATHARNA (*haughtily*).

My innocence gives strength to meet the charge.

(*Satirically.*)

But why are all your followers well armed?
In dread of women's bodkins? I'll prepare,
With your permission, to accompany you,
Cloaking in the adjoining room.

MALCHUS.

I fear
I must constrain you to depart at once.
Hanno commanded me emphatically
Not to lose sight of you.

KATHARNA (*haughtily*).

I hold your name
A guarantee for courteous treatment, sir.

(*Persuasively.*)

Pray send a trusted messenger with me ;
Then, duly habited with shawl and hood,
I'll hasten to repel this cruel charge,
And prove to Hanno my sincerity.

MALCHUS.

Madam, delay not long, for Hanno waits :
Abdalonim, attend the lady hence.

(*Exeunt* KATHARNA *and* ABDALONIM, *through curtains, into an adjoining apartment.* MALCHUS
addresses MUTHUMBAL.)

A fascinating dame, no doubt of it !
Did you observe her mien when first we came ?
Like that of some proud warrior chief beset,
And driven to bay within his last redoubt.
Then pleased with our appearance she became
In face and manner most agreeable,
Till by degrees the pleasant semblance rose,
We were allies and long-tried friends of old.
Now, good Muthumbal, I can understand
The subtle magnet of a woman's eye,
Which tames the sterner temper of our sex,
Rendering our conduct fair and courteous ;
But still I cannot comprehend the power
That duped great Hanno, bound his yielding will,
Forced him to stultify his policy,
Sending Hasdrubal, though he had opposed
Till then his marching into Italy !

     (A pause, after which MALCHUS *continues*
       satirically.)

Methinks the lady trifles far too long !
Perhaps attires herself with tricky skill,
And smoothened niceness, to uphold her sway
Where first she conquered.

      *(*MALCHUS *calls through the curtain.)*
       Pardon, madam, pray ;
But we must now proceed.

    (No answer being returned, MALCHUS *bursts through*
   the curtains, and is then heard to exclaim.)
       Abdalonim !
Great Moloch's Face ! !   The Countenance of Baal ! ! !

       *(*MALCHUS *returns.)*

Our noble quarry's gone !   Abdalonim
Lies helpless, gagged and bound, in mute reproach ;
Chained like a felon by Camilla's slaves,
Who, fearing punishment, have swiftly fled.

(MALCHUS *addresses two of his followers.*)

Release the good Abdalonim at once.

(*Exeunt the two followers, as directed.*   MALCHUS
continues, addressing other followers.)

Guard quick the gates !   Grant heaven 'tis not too late !

(*Exeunt hurriedly, on both sides, the followers
addressed.*)

For dreadful is the Suffete's darker mood,
Both fierce and deadly, as when lightning flames
Down from the storm-clouds on the helpless earth,
And scorches midst the din of warring spheres.
But if the bird is flown, at least her nest
Remains your proper prize.

MUTHUMBAL.

No further hint
Is needed, sir ; they're like the eager hounds
That spurn the leash to chase the flying deer !

(*Exeunt all except* MUTHUMBAL, *who continues,
pointing over his shoulder with his thumb after*
MALCHUS.)

She duped poor Malchus while he laughed at ease,
Deeming it safe where Hanno was ensnared.
Ha ! ha ! 'tis wiser not to take as guide,

In weighty matters, any woman's smile.
That was the reason why Malchus was pleased,

(*Drawing himself up.*)

Having reliance on *my* self-control,
That I should court fair Hercta once again ;
He hoped her prattle might perhaps disclose
Some useful secrets, if they should exist,
Touching Camilla and the Suffete's flame ;
And though I own myself aglow with love,
It would be strange indeed if I advised
With charming Hercta on affairs of state,
Whispering their confidences in her ear !
Although she is a very clever girl,
Much interested in what touches me.

(*A pause.*)

How she enjoys the quiet, skilful moves,
By which I guide old Malchus safe along,
And lead him where I wish, but still conceal
The strings by which I move the puppet-show,
Whose figures tickle him and point the road !

(*He exclaims.*)

But stay !

(*Speaking slowly, in perplexity.*)

I told my Hercta that the mob
This evening would invade Camilla's house.

(*Defiantly.*)

But what of that ?   It was to save her life !
And she is most discreet, in silence safe.

No doubt she locked the secret in her breast,
And fled in time to shun the risk of ill.

(*Contentedly.*)

So she will come to-morrow to the tryst ;
May Tanit's blessing rest upon her head !

(*Exit.*)

ACT IV.

SCENE I.

Courtyard of ELISSA'S *palace, situated at some days'
journey from Carthage. Enter* King MASSINISSA
accompanied by two courtiers.

MASSINISSA (*dubiously*).

I fear my eagerness, which spurred me on,
Has brought me somewhat early in the day:
For my return to urge my suit again,
After the war in which my fortunes failed;
But it is now too late to hesitate.

(A pause.)

Quickness is best in changeful times like these,
When war may summon any warrior
To seek the field of battle in an hour.
Now peace gives liberty for tender words,
Breathed softly in a-lady's little ear:
With tender glances from love-laden eyes,
And thrilling pressures of the lingering lips.

(He knocks at the castle door.)

But who comes here? King Sphax to thwart again!
Sent by an evil genius, certainly.

(Enter King SPHAX, attended by two courtiers.)

My service to your highness.

> (*The two kings and their attendants bow
> low to each other.*)

SPHAX.

Gracious lord,
As ruler of a country bordering yours,
I seize this opportunity to tell
My happiness, that all our strife is past.
May peace for ever reign between our states !

MASSINISSA.

Such is my earnest prayer !

SPHAX (*aside*).

Unfortunate !
Forced thus to parley here on even terms ;
Although the conqueror, doomed to enter last,
All's lost if he should gain first audience !
How could a maiden care for argument
From one grown old and sere, however wise,
When nature's promptings have persuaded her
To listen to the warmer words of love
Breathed by a rival ?

> (*The castle door is opened by a Slave : he looks with
> hesitation from one party of visitors to the other,
> as they stand collected on either side of the door.
> SPHAX continues addressing MASSINISSA.*)

Will your highness grant
That I may enter first?

MASSINISSA (*indignantly*).

My time's short, sir :
How do you base this claim?

SPHAX.

Upon the war.

MASSINISSA.

First comers take the *pas.*

SPHAX.

My victory
By chance has given precedence to me now ;
Though mine is not a greater worthiness,
Except through fickle fortune.

MASSINISSA.

Still, I hold,
We meet as nobles here, and not as kings
Enthroned.

SPHAX (*persuasively*).

Then yield precedence to my years.

MASSINISSA (*laughing*).

'Tis the first time, unless you only jest,
That age has been advanced as forming claims
Within the sunny courts of youthful love :
At least I never knew it so !

SPHAX (*angrily*).

No, boy !
No, beardless boy, the wonder is not great :
But rather that you have known anything,
Besides experience of some childish toys !

MASSINISSA (*drawing his sword*).

Hah, insolence indeed !   A plaything this,
I warrant I have not forgot to use.
Come, draw, sir, draw !

> (SPHAX *draws his sword and they fight ; the courtiers*
> *on either side also draw their weapons and*
> *engage.*)

SLAVE.

They fight within the gates !
I'll close the door at once, and bear the news
To Dame Elissa.

> (*The Slave re-enters, and closes the door.   A window*
> *of the palace overlooking the gate is hastily opened,*
> *and* Dame ELISSA *appears at it.*)

ELISSA.

Pause, your highnesses!
I do beseech you both to stay your hands,
Nor bring ill-fortune to my widowed home,
Beyond the evil that the gods have willed
Already in my husband's death!

(*The combatants pause, and draw back a little
beyond engaging distance.*)

SPHAX.

Madam,
Your presence calms, like oil upon the waves.

ELISSA.

I thank your highness, on my own part,
And from my daughter, for your courtesy
In coming here to-day. I grieve to say
The Lady Sophonisba is unwell :
This bars the pleasure of receiving you ;
But on her earliest recovery
She will invite one of your highnesses,
Through me, to come again and hear her thanks,
With full permission given to urge his suit ;
Till then, your highnesses, farewell !

SPHAX AND MASSINISSA.

Farewell !
(*Exit* ELISSA.)

MASSINISSA.

Your highness, we shall meet again.

SPHAX.

Elsewhere :
When you appoint, you will not find me fail !

(*The two parties bow to each other, and withdraw
in opposite directions.   Exeunt.*)

SCENE II.

Reception-room in the palace of ELISSA.   SOPHONISBA
engaged in arranging flowers in a vase.   Enter
ELISSA.

ELISSA (*aside*).

I must not frighten her with vivid tales,
Of Sphax and Massinissa fighting here,
But gloss it over.

(*Aloud.*)

Sophonisba, dear ;
Believe me it is most desirable
That you should soon decide between the suits
Of the two Western kings who came to-day,
Seeking your answers which will seal their fate.
They do high honour to our family,
While paying tribute to your loveliness.

By chance they met this morning at our gates,
And found bitter excuse to disagree,
But listened to my soothing words of peace;
As well behoved such courteous gentlemen,
Appealed to by a lady.

SOPHONISBA.

Marriage, now?
O mother, would the matter were postponed!
The thought weighs on my spirit like a spell;
That I might soon be called on to leave home,
And live amid the wars.

ELISSA.

Grieve not for this;
But as you may desire, so it shall be:
And I, your only parent, will approve.
Yet if, of free consent, you could accept
The offer of a husband and a crown,
Why, Carthage then would secure an ally;
While now, although hard-pressed in Africa,
She cannot count on either king.

SOPHONISBA.

Well, well!
Dear mother, as you wish, I'll think of it.

(*Aside.*)

It seems my country's cause requires my aid;
Or else I would not wed with either lord.

Which should I choose ?   The venerable Sphax,
Who would soon free me from my bond again ;
Or youthful Massinissa for my life ?
So, to the end, my heart might throb in vain
For freedom ; as the panting, captured bird,
Caught in the fowler's cruel net.

(Enter a Slave.)

SLAVE (addressing ELISSA).

Madam,

A city lady begs an interview,
For though she wears a fortune-teller's dress,
She speaks as one who dwells in palaces ;
Not like the poor who ply the mystic trade,
And sleep at night beneath the starry heavens.
She would relate some weighty business,
Petitioning for aid.

ELISSA.

Return at once :

Conduct her here with kindly courtesy.
(Exit Slave, who presently returns with KATHARNA,
who is dressed as a fortune-teller.   Exit Slave.)

KATHARNA (to ELISSA).

Madam, believe me, driven by great distress
To venture this intrusion on your time ;
Which, pardon me, as thus I hope to save
A prize to woman dearer than her life,
From the dread menace of a man I hate.

Elissa.

Already you have said enough to win
My sympathy, with one in urgent need ;
Who asks a sister's help to shield her fame.
I pray disclose your name? Who is the wretch
Who persecutes you ?

Katharna.

Madam, by my birth
A Spaniard, I have dwelt for many years
In Carthage, and Camilla is my name ;
While he who would ensnare me in his toils
Is Suffete Hanno.

Sophonisba.

Fortune favours me,
In that it brings Camilla to my side,
Although her troubles grieve me to the heart ;
For often I have heard from eager lips
The praise of one whose charms and virtues vied,
Each rivalling each in greater excellence.

Elissa.

Still stronger is the claim you hold on me,
To save you from the crafty Suffete's power,
Hostile to you and to my family.
Accept, I pray, a sanctuary here,
Until safer retreats are found for you,
And ever deem me pledged to aid your cause.

Since household business summons me away,
Be pleased to pardon if I leave you now,
With commendations, to my daughter's care.

KATHARNA.

Madam,
My gratitude is deep for all you grant ;
Well worthy is this hospitality
Of your famed justice and benevolence,
Which tempted me to seek protection here ;
The more that I knew well your husband's power
Was used against the Suffete Hanno.

ELISSA.

Yes ;
Peace be with him : my husband ever chose
The wisest course to gain his country's good !

(*Exit* ELISSA.)

SOPHONISBA.

Now we're alone I wish to ask a boon
From one who bears the mystic signs of lore,
Dark divination and the magic spells ;
Pray tell a maid in sore perplexity,
Wooed by two suitors, if her choice should fall
On one of them.

KATHARNA.

I'd aid you willingly ;
But, madam, know this strange and tawdry garb

Is but a cloak to frail humanity ;
Nor would I trade upon your offered trust
By arrogating powers I do not own.
But if your fancy wishes from a seer,
The mere embroidery of a useful robe,
Pray learn my thoughts which prompt the following lines

Not he whose youth and beauty please the eye
Will prove the firmest friend if need shall try :
But he who lately led his valiant hosts
To glorious victory on the Western coasts.

SOPHONISBA (*smiling*).

Your modesty disclaims the magic power :
And yet my suitors are both known to you !
Well, your rhyme points this moral to the tale :
That I should choose the stronger in the field,
And bind him firmly, as a sure ally
To aid my country.

KATHARNA.

Madam, it is so ;
I have no knowledge but a woman's thoughts :
And yet perhaps I know more subtle things
Than those who with a solemn mien pretend
To wield the wand of witchcraft.

SOPHONISBA.

That is well :
You will enlighten me as I require ;

Be sure we shall discuss the matter more
When leisure bids ; but now I must retire
To aid my dearest mother, if she needs.
I pray you rest after your journey's toil,
Securely here.

KATHARNA.

I thank your ladyship.

(*Exit* SOPHONISBA.)

An amiable girl, who has deserved
My deepest gratitude.   Ah, would that she
Might live in happiness and peace, as now :
A flower ungathered on the parent stem !
Nor do her suitors move her heart or mind,
Else she would not require a stranger's aid
To judge the merits of their tales of love.
But policy compelled me to promote
Her marriage schemes, to gain in Africa
The vantage we have lost in Italy.
Yet my rhymed choice may well be true enough,
To judge by Massinissa's shifty eye,
And Spax's tempered, kind complacency,
That lacks not firmness when there is a need,
Being well-suited to hold close in check,
And rule the fiery passions of a man,
Which make youth fickle but old age secure,
To her who first may win the suitor's love.
But here comes Hercta, who I must release
From her long faithful services.

(*Enter* HERCTA.)

                                          At last,
Dear Hercta, you are free to leave me here,
Where I am welcomed with kind courtesy,
By Dame Elissa's and her daughter's grace,
Until this momentary need is past ;
Though I might dwell for ever here in peace,
Or wander soon perhaps to other scenes,
Seeking oblivion from my lasting cares.
Return, then, to your lover, who would wed,
And live in happiness as you deserve,
Remembering always in your distant home
My gratitude for your great services
Will never fade.   I owe you more than life ;
For through your warning I escaped the snare
That Hanno and his agents spread.

    (KATHARNA *offers her hand, which* HERCTA *kisses.*)

HERCTA.

                                        Madam,
I trust that you may live in happiness,
Enjoying health and all prosperity ;
And if by chance you should have need of me,
Summon, and I will hasten to your side,
Esteeming it a happy privilege
To serve my valued mistress once again.

               (*Exit* HERCTA.)

KATHARNA.

Indeed, fate trifles with our happiness !
Think of my youthful days, long past, in Spain,

When I was Hannibal's affianced wife,
Blessed by a father's and a sister's love.
What have I now to hope for in my life?
Some vengeance I have had, 'tis true, on Rome ;
Complete revenge, for which I yielded all,
Is long in its fulfilment, if it come.
But Hercta, left an orphan by the wars,
Was never led to quit a woman's sphere
Of modest, tender usefulness and love :
Now reaps her just reward, a happy home.

(*She weeps.*)

In her I lose my oldest, truest friend,
Who dwelt since childhood ever at my side.

(*Exit* KATHARNA.)

SCENE III.

Before the Senate-house in Carthage. Enter HANNIBAL
*on his way to the Senate ; a mob gathers, cheering
him, bowing, and gesticulating.*

HANNIBAL.

My friends, I thank you for your welcoming ;
But moderate the honours you bestow :
Cheer louder when I vanquish Scipio,
And drive his troops from Carthaginian soil.
Remember, 'tis your work as well as mine !

(HANNIBAL *enters the Senate-house. Exeunt the
crowd cheering. Presently enter* HANNO *in his
palanquin, accompanied by* MALCHUS. HANNO
alights. Exeunt the bearers with the litter.)

HANNO.

Well, have you any further word of her ?
What happened when Katharna had escaped
So narrowly ?

MALCHUS.

As yet there is no news :
But we are making careful search, my lord.
The rabble quickly wrecked the lady's house,
Though plundering seemed to whet their appetites,
Not to appease the wrath we had aroused,
Which waxed and spread like fierce, devouring flames,
First kindled from a spark, and bursting soon
Beyond control.   Katharna, sir, has fled ;
And we may deem ourselves most fortunate
Can we but quell the furious storm we raised
To bring about her capture.

HANNO.

Pooh, my friend !
The mob may be enraged, but dare not move
As long as I can sway the Senators.
Heed not their chatter, which assails the ear
As ripened carrion assaults the nose,
And though offensive, does as little harm
To any one.

(*Enter an insurgent mob, armed with sticks,
stones, and weapons.*)

FIRST INSURGENT.

Come on, we'll seize him now.

SECOND INSURGENT.

The vixen has escaped, but here's the fox !

(*The mob seize* HANNO, *and also* MALCHUS.)

HANNO.

Hold off your hands : I'll pension liberally
Whoever rescues me !

FIRST INSURGENT.

Well done, my men :
Our fortune favours, there are two of them !
And both deserving——

(*Enter* MUTHUMBAL.)

SECOND INSURGENT.

Oh, look out, my friends :
There's now a third from the same rookery !

(*Some of the mob move towards* MUTHUMBAL *with
a view to seizing him.*)

FIRST INSURGENT.

Come back ! Avoid the scribe, whose scholar's art
Betokens dealings with the devil.

THIRD INSURGENT.

Yes ;
His restless spirit might disturb our nights !

FOURTH INSURGENT.

Two victims are enough !

MUTHUMBAL (*aside*).

I'll call the guard.

(*Exit* MUTHUMBAL.)

MALCHUS.

It was Katharna's crime ; for she bewitched,
Through fiendish powers bestowed by foreign gods,
The Suffete's better judgment.   We deplore
As much as you the terrible mischance ;
But all we may achieve by remedies
Shall instantly be done ; and now beware,
For if you do not quickly set us free,
Swift punishment will reach you as deserved ;
But let us go, and you shall be excused
Upon the plea that some misguided zeal
Had warped your reason until we explained
That we were blameless but unfortunate.

(*Aside.*)

When once we're rescued 'twill be different :
And they shall suffer for their insolence,
The ringleaders by death.

THIRD INSURGENT.

Yes, comrades, stay :
Hanno thought best to serve our country's good
By sending out Hasdrubal and his force ;
The measure failed, but he was not to blame ;
That is my view.

FOURTH INSURGENT.

He should have sacrificed
As he had promised, giving holiday.
And not by trifling tantalise the god,
Until he slaughtered all our hardiest troops,
To recompense him for the public loss
Of his due honours.

FIRST INSURGENT.

All might have been well
If he had sacrificed and kept his word :
He promised us a general holiday
And lighter taxes ; yet he changed his plans
To please his fancy and a foreigner,
Who might wish ill to Carthage any day ;
And if 'tis true that she bewitched his mind,
He was unfortunate but still in fault,
So he must suffer for the public good.

SECOND INSURGENT.

Yes, for he merits death !

OTHER INSURGENTS.

And Malchus too !

SECOND INSURGENT.

Where shall we slay them ?

FOURTH INSURGENT.

They deserve the cross !

(*The sound of a distant trumpet is heard.*)

FIRST INSURGENT.

Hark to the trumpet sounding the alarm :
Soldiers will hurry here to rescue them :
Time presses !

SECOND INSURGENT.

Bear them to the battlements,
And hurl the cunning traitors headlong thence !

FIRST INSURGENT.

Well said ! Away with them !

OTHER INSURGENTS (*entering hurriedly.*)

The troops ! The troops !

FOURTH INSURGENT.

Quick, quick ! Lead on !

VOICES FROM THE CROWD.

Away ! Lead on ! Away !

(*Excunt the mob, dragging* HANNO *and* MALCHUS.
Re-enter MUTHUMBAL, *followed by an Officer
leading a company of soldiers.*)

MUTHUMBAL (*excitedly.*)

I fear the mob, knowing their time is short,
May do the mischief faster.

OFFICER.

                    Yet, be sure,
My men will give a good account of them,
And all their leaders shall be put to death ;
Caught thus red-handed, doing violence
To Hanno and a Suffete's dignity !

MUTHUMBAL.

We must do more, for it behoves to save
Two valued lives in greatest jeopardy.

(*Exeunt hurriedly, following the crowd.*)

SCENE IV.

Throne-room in SPHAX'S *palace. Courtiers conversing in groups, awaiting the King's arrival.* PARIHU *and two courtiers form a group in front.*

PARIHU.

Everything was successful ; and the sun
Shone, with bright hope for these dominions,
Upon the crowds and pageantry displayed
In honour of the marriage of the King.
When, from the temple's porch, their Highnesses
Came forth to mount the elephants of state,
How joyously the people thronged around :
With warmest welcomes offered to our lord
And lovely Sophonisba.

FIRST COURTIER.

It is well
That a fair consort should enjoy the throne :
Who, with a woman's care and tenderness,
May gently influence her husband's mind ;
Ameliorating much the people's lot
In times of famine and distress.

(The Hunchback joins the group.)

THE HUNCHBACK.

News ! News !
My lieges, I bring news——

SECOND COURTIER.

Surely you jest !

THE HUNCHBACK.

If I did make a joke 'twas not my first :
And if I boasted, I but followed out
A motto which I framed in early youth ;
For thus it ran :—

Your trumpet always blow :
Unless perchance you can
Persuade some other man
To advertise your show.

SECOND COURTIER.

You do it well :
Having had much experience in the art.

THE HUNCHBACK.

Yes, truly ; most men are too much engaged
In chanting their own praises, to attend
Or spare me their assistance for my tune ;
While some are occupied in picking holes
In others' coats.

(*He nods significantly towards the second courtier
who turns away disdainfully.*)

FIRST COURTIER.

Pray, what may be your news?

THE HUNCHBACK.

I'll state what *is* my news, by your kind leave.
First, Hanno has been slain in a street brawl,
Or sudden rising of a faction mob.
Next, Carthage has recalled the lion's brood,
Hamilcar's sons, to defend Africa
Against the troops of wily Scipio,
Whose army threatens at her city gates.
But word has come of gallant Mago's death,
From wounds lately received at Genoa.
He breathed his last when traversing the sea,
And died : the only thing he ever did
Of which I disapprove !

FIRST COURTIER.

Who brought the news?

THE HUNCHBACK.

I heard a messenger inform the King.
Mago is blameless ; doubtless he'd have lived
Had it been possible.

SECOND COURTIER.

If tired of life,
You would not have refused his fixed desire,

And doomed him without favour or excuse,
A jaded man to walk a weary world ?

THE HUNCHBACK.

No one may die unless he wish to live.

SECOND COURTIER.

Explain your meaning ?

THE HUNCHBACK.

For example now :
If king and country have decreed his death,
Or send him journeying for the nation's good
Where rigorous winters mercilessly scourge,
Fierce scorching suns and winds asphyxiate,
Or where the niggard earth withholds her yield,
And exile means destruction.

SECOND COURTIER (*drily*).

Very true ;
" Happy despatch," his fate might then be called !

THE HUNCHBACK.

That hinges on his nationality.
Look eastward :—How the folks in Russia *
Despatch whole crowds but never happily !
Look west :—There lie the favoured British Isles :
Whose people, always happy, ne'er despatch !
At least so say the Punic mariners :

* *N. B.*—The anachronism here, as to name and fact, is of course
intentional.

Who go, attracted by the mines of tin,
To barter Carthaginian merchandise
For the rich ores found in the rocky earth,
And amber gathered on the Baltic coasts—
The tempest-beaten ocean's frozen foam ;
Sure talisman for witchcraft and disease,
A valued gem and brilliant ornament.

                                        (*A pause.*)

They deem the British women beautiful,
Who yet prefer to wed their countrymen
Rather than mate with any foreigners ;
But this the Carthaginian sailors hold
A proof of very strange and faulty taste
In matrimonial matters.

                FIRST COURTIER.

                        Yes, no doubt :
'Tis natural for disappointed men,
Esteeming highly their own worthiness,
To wish the heavens were green instead of blue !
Pray how does Carthage city prosper ?

            THE HUNCHBACK (*significantly*).

                        O-o-o-oh !
Why there the wealthy merchant citizens
Place profit before all.   Believe me, sirs,
There is no outrage or atrocity
Which they cannot achieve by means of gold.
Meanwhile they bear themselves most jauntily,
As having right and justice on their side :

And loudly they proclaim their ends in view
Are freedom, science, progress, or the good
Of some one else, but never of themselves.
What villainies they order they ignore ;
While the poor tools, through whom they gain their
    ends,
Have sold themselves to Satan, without choice :
For hunger's a hard master !

FIRST COURTIER.

Very bad !

THE HUNCHBACK (*sententiously*).

Bad for good men : but without carrion
There'd be no food for crows !

SECOND COURTIER.

You've croaked enough !
Have you no good news to dilute the ill ?

THE HUNCHBACK.

Yes : Hannibal has landed on the coast,
And now gathers his gallant troops in haste,
To bar the onward march of Scipio.
    (*A third courtier joins the group, in time to hear the
        Hunchback's last reply.*)

THIRD COURTIER.

A pleasing prospect truly : yet there lowers
On our horizon a portentous cloud ;
For word is now brought by a courier

That Massinissa calls his state to arms.
But who can tell his secret purposes?
Whether he will turn eastward at the news
That Hannibal is on the Punic coast,
Or, plunging midst the woods, the swamps and wastes,
Will he emerge upon us suddenly,
Hoping to find our army unprepared,
And snatch a victory through our tardiness?
Therefore I say, good sirs, that if no war
Arise to overshadow all our joy,
We may esteem it fortunate.

FIRST COURTIER.

                Grave news ;
But let us hope that fate will favour us :
And as the mountain draws the thunder-cloud,
So Hannibal attracts him to the east.

    (*Enter* SPHAX, *leading* SOPHONISBA *by the hand,*
        with respectful affection. He conducts her to the
        thrones, where they seat themselves side by side.
        The courtiers bow low as the royal couple pass,
        and then await the King's pleasure.)

SPHAX.

I thank you for your noble escort, sirs ;
And that in martial courtesy you brought
Warriors and elephants to swell my train.
And now we bid you all, my lords, farewell!

    (*The nobles and courtiers bow. Exeunt all except*
        SPHAX *and* SOPHONISBA. SPHAX *continues.*)

A pleasing duty thus to register
Throughout the morning many a friendly vow,
With loyal prayers breathed for our happiness.
And now, my love, accept from me, I pray,
My warmest welcome to these ancient halls,
Which henceforth are your home ; while I remain
Your firm-devoted lover, friend, and slave,

(*Smiling.*)

Your husband and parental guardian.

(*He bows to* SOPHONISBA.)

SOPHONISBA.

Your kindness moves me, sir, beyond all words
Which I might feebly use in gratitude ;
I will implore the gods for health and strength,
That I may tend you with a daughter's care,
And bring conjugal happiness——

(*Enter a Messenger, hurriedly.*)

MESSENGER.

My liege,
I come to warn you thus in hottest haste,
That Massinissa marches on the coast :
While his armed galleys lash the sea to foam,
And bear his lines prolonged upon the waves.
So eager is his mood, he hastens here
With cavalry, to strike an earlier blow,
And has already hurried far ahead
Of his main army.

SPHAX.

Youth was ever rash.
'Tis well ; now summon all the gallant chiefs
Who led my conquering troops but yesterday
Against this young marauder.   By the aid
Of the immortal gods, vouchsafed before,
My host again shall triumph.   Send me here
A laurel-wreath prepared to crown my brows
On my return, when the good citizens
Will bring congratulations.

MESSENGER.

Yes, my liege.

(*Exit Messenger.*)

SPHAX.

May his impatience prove his final doom ;
For, if he hurries on, almost alone,
To meet him first and then his following troops,
Is better than to fight with both combined.

(*Enter an Officer bearing a wreath of laurels which
he hands, with an obeisance, to* SPHAX, *who
places it upon a small table.   Exit Officer.*)

SPHAX (*to* SOPHONISBA).

I leave this wreath at hand, and before long
You shall enhance its worth by placing it

Upon a conqueror's brow ; and now, farewell !
I give you, dearest, into Tanit's care !

(*He kisses her forehead.*)

SOPHONISBA.

I pray good fortune may attend you, sir !

(*Exit* SPHAX *hurriedly.*)

I would that dear Katharna were with me,
Then I should feel less lonely when the King
Is absent at the wars or else the chase,
As doubtless he will often need to be.
And when the urgent matters are complete
That called her back to Carthage on the news
Of Hanno's death, she will return again ;
For as she journeyed hence she pledged her word.
May she come soon !   I must have patience now.

(*Exit.*)

SCENE V.

The gardens of HANNIBAL'S *palace at Carthage. Enter*
KATHARNA, *disguised as a fortune-teller. Her hair
falls down over the forehead : and as her shawl, which
passes over her head, is drawn across a considerable
portion of her face, little more than the eyes remain
uncovered.*

KATHARNA (*turning suddenly*).

Ah, Hannibal approaches !   Would that now
I might make myself known, perhaps retrieve

Our happiness, in this one interview ;
But I must wait till cruel Rome is crushed.
The object must be followed while there's hope :
When none remains, I'll bide till peace is won.
So in the coming interview with him,
Help me, ye gods, to bear an even mien
And curb emotion !

> (*Enter* HANNIBAL, *on his way to the Senate.*
> KATHARNA *addresses him.*)
> Mighty Hannibal,

The noble champion of Africa
And Carthage !   Though Rome still is unsubdued,
It fires my ardent blood to think of all
The many glorious triumphs of your wars !
O would that I had been at least a man,
To join the march, the bivouac, the fight,
Or offer help as humblest of your slaves :
To live or die as careless fate might choose,
Yet highly favoured in the sacrifice :
As trodden mounds are honoured if they bore
A chief whose mind controlled winged Victory !

HANNIBAL.

Good woman, yours are worthy words indeed :
So speak true patriots ; yet your garb denotes
An alien origin ?

KATHARNA.

'Tis true ; I come
From Tingis and the Gates of Hercules,

To ply my trade of telling fortunes here,
Attracted by the Carthaginian wealth ;
But midst the busy throng I dwell alone :

(She falters.)

No father's care nor husband's loving arm
Protects, sustains, and guides me on my way.

(She recovers composure.)

Yet if·you wish convincing evidence
Of my deep knowledge of the darker powers,
Know that your feud with Rome, like the forked tongue
Of the fierce cobra, bears a double point !
While one is urged by patriotic zeal,
The other burns to wreak a dire revenge
For private wrongs inflicted on a friend.

(HANNIBAL, *who was beginning to move away, starts,
turns, and scrutinises her for a moment.*)

HANNIBAL.

It may be as you say, for who records
The complex workings of his inner mind ?

(A pause.)

Do you know aught of those of whom you hint ?

KATHARNA.

I am not yet allowed to raise the veil
That shrouds the future of the one you love.

(She pauses : then aside.)

He hazards no denial that his flame
Still burns for me !

(*Aloud.*)

But shining through the gloom
And fiercely threatening turmoil of the times,
With Scipio gathering his troops and fleets
To war with Carthage on her native coasts :
I see a day appear when once again,
Your grasp shall press the hand of her you love.

HANNIBAL (*earnestly*).

Great Melkarth grant it ! Now I must be gone :
The Senate waits.

(*Exit* HANNIBAL.)

KATHARNA.

Thank heaven that he is true !

(*She sinks on her knees, burying her face
in her hands. Curtain.*)

Scene VI.

Reception-room in Sphax's *palace.* Enter Massinissa *hurriedly, followed by* Sophonisba : *he sees the laurel-wreath.*

Massinissa.

A laurel-wreath prepared ! Most courteous !

(*He hands the wreath to* Sophonisba, *and bends his head down so that she may adjust it : thus he does not observe her look of surprise and pain as she complies with his request.*)

Madam, it happened thus :—The rival host,
Led on by Sphax himself, had hurried out
To take advantage of my scattered march :
Through haste, neglecting search for ambushes ;
But I was warned in time by trusty scouts,
And met their front with quickly gathered force :
Except a chosen legion, which I sent,
Concealed by woods, onto the southern side ;
Where it rushed forth upon the struggling flank
Of the foes, shaken by their fight with me
In front, hurling them northwards on the coast ;
There from my boats and ships the arrows showered,
To slay them fast in spite of helm and shield :
Until the fall of Sphax, who sought in vain
To rally once again his shattered troops,

But died a glorious death and sealed the day,
My victory.

SOPHONISBA (*weeping*).

My lord, excuse my grief ;
Alas, I mourn the venerable Sphax :
Who e'er was tender in his love for me,
And chivalrous.

MASSINISSA.

If that be so, indeed,
Then for your sake, dear lady, I as well
Regard his memory with gratitude.
And yet you were the prize whose influence
Inspired me to this triumph, otherwise
I would not have tried fate again so soon,
Against a foe of late victorious :
For had I failed, my smaller realm was lost
By annexation to his territory ;
But now his states are mine, this is my home ;
I need but your consent, for which I crave,
To crown my happiness on such a day :
Rewarding my devotion and my love
With bright connubial blessings.

SOPHONISBA (*in gentle entreaty*).

Grant me time,
That I may give consideration due

To such a weighty matter ; and excuse
My lack of ready words to thank your grace,
Amid the echo of your questioning.

MASSINISSA (*imploringly*).

Speak now the word that will decide my fate !

(*He sinks on his knees before her and extends his
hands to receive hers.*)

SOPHONISBA (*aside*).

My grief for Sphax would prompt me to decline,
But duty bids me win a sword from Rome.

(*She approaches and places her hand in his.*)

My lonely weakness yields——

MASSINISSA.

Thank heaven for that !
Madam, if you consent, that is enough ;
I am most joyful.

SOPHONISBA.

Now I beg of you
For courteous delay : from reverence
To Sphax's memory.

MASSINISSA.

Madam, I agree ;
But pardon my impatience when I hope
The time may be as short as possible :
And deem it a just tribute to your charms
That I should wish an early marriage day.

(*Curtain.*)

ACT V.

Scene I.

Before the tent of Scipio, *in the Roman camp near Carthage ; on one side there stands a small stone altar to Jupiter. Enter from the tent* Scipio.

Scipio.

That Massinissa is ambitious, young,
And fickle, well I know.   He shall be plied
With specious arguments and promises ;
But if they fail or prove to lack in force,
Then I will feign the supernatural
And win by necromancy, in pretence.

> (*Enter a Magician from Egypt, ushered in by an Officer, who withdraws.*)

Magician (*solemnly*).

You summoned me in haste, and I am here,
Prepared to do your bidding, and command
Dark spirits in the earth and ocean deep
To war in your behalf, and exercise
Strong influence upon the minds of men, .
Till they believe what you desire.

SCIPIO.

                                    Good sir,
I readily accept your services,
And give you this in earnest of reward ;

                          (SCIPIO *gives him money.*)

Yet fourfold greater shall your guerdon be,
If you successfully achieve the task
As I require : and guard its secresy ;
But save your boast of wielding magic powers
To dazzle other minds than Scipio's :

                                    (*Smiling.*)

Reserve it for moon-gazers and the like,
Who, finding not enough of mystery
In the plain order of the universe,
Conceive that feeble man can thwart its rules
And make its powers obey his wanton will
By a mere turn of thought !   But time draws on :
Then know that presently, ere twilight falls,
There comes a native prince to visit me,
Whom I would fain impress by mystic lore
To deem me as the chosen of the gods,
So that he may adopt my policy.
Each time I wish for a portentous sign
I will approach and touch this altar-stone ;
Which being as a signal meant for you,
While you stand watching, hidden on the hill :
Then wield the powers which fiction gives the gods,
And burst the rocks above with chemicals,
The make of which magicians know full well,
Instructed by the wizards of Cathay :

The sound will echo through the mountain-tops,
That all may think Jove thunders in his wrath
At what I disapprove.

THE MAGICIAN (*smiling*).

           It shall be done
As you desire, my lord.

SCIPIO.

               I can rely
Upon your skill and judgment.
           (*Exit Magician. Enter an Officer.*)

SCIPIO.

                  Well, what news ?
How say the scouts and spies in their reports ?

OFFICER.

My lord, they bring no further word as yet,
Beyond that first received ; that Hannibal
Consolidates his force and bides his time,
Making no movement from his vantage ground
Under protection of the city walls ;
But levying, arming, drilling, day by day,
Fresh bands of citizens unused to war,
And who would need some years of discipline
To make them worthy foemen.

SCIPIO.

It is well :
I have foreseen this and prepared my plans ;
Give orders that we march at break of day
To wait the enemy on Zama's plain.
Send the Chief Augur to me.

OFFICER.

Yes, my lord.
                    (*Exit Officer.*)

SCIPIO.

Thus, by my challenge, I may tempt him on,
So far beyond the shelter of his walls,
When he is ready to encounter me,
That if I conquer I'll destroy his force.;
While if he hesitates to take the gage
That, in advancing, I hurl at his feet,
His troops will be downcast, and mine inspired,
And so my way prepared for victory.
          (*Enter an Officer ushering in the Chief Augur :
                 the Officer then withdraws.*)

AUGUR.

I come, my lord, to learn what you command ;
Which, be my head the forfeit, shall be done
As you direct.

SCIPIO.

To-morrow we move hence
To Zama's plains : there offer sacrifice
To all the gods, but most to Jupiter ;
And having scrutinised the burning flesh,
Proclaim yourself enabled to foretell
That victory will attend us in the war :
This quickly spreading, passed from mouth to mouth
Will raise high confidence amongst the troops,
Making our triumph all the more assured ;
For faith gives courage and begets the strength
To firmly strive to reach the wished-for goal,
Till failure withers on its shrunken stalk,
And bright success becomes a certain prize.
I close in battle with full confidence :
My Roman citizens are soldiers born ;
And every one of them has volunteered—
A system which selects the bold and strong,
And those best suited to a martial life.
Besides, the offering of his services
Makes of a man a hero in his heart,
Raising the warrior on a pinnacle,
Till emulation, spreading through the land,
Fills with ripe courage timid breasts at last.
So I know well my gallant men are staunch ;
Yet Hannibal no longer leads the Gauls
And Spanish troops, who fought in Italy,
But a mere rabble hastily equipped,
Composed of native Carthaginians :
Good merchandisers and not men of war,

Compelled to join the ranks against their will.
Thus cowed by being driven, and made to loathe
The warfare which by nature they disliked,
And hitherto ingloriously shunned
By paying foreigners to fight for them,
Until the canker softness so ingrew,
Sapping their manliness and energies
As dry-rot crumbles e'en the firmest wood,
That now it threats to overwhelm their state,
Which seeks protection from their palsied arms,
And lies defenceless through its sons' decay.
So prophesy they fail.

AUGUR.

I will, my lord.

(*Exit Augur.   Enter a Roman Officer.*)

OFFICER.

My lord, King Massinissa has arrived.

SCIPIO.

Conduct his Highness now, to me.

OFFICER.

Yes, sir.

(*Exit Officer, who presently ushers in* King
MASSINISSA, *and then withdraws.*)

SCIPIO.

Ah, Massinissa, you are welcome here !
And I have needed much to speak with you ;
Therefore I told my wish by messenger,
Which you with courtesy have gratified.
Word of your marriage has been brought to me,
Which I would fain regard as happy news
And see alone in it domestic joys ;
But you have wed the daughter of our foe,
A Carthaginian general, who fell
Not long ago in arms against our power :
This saps the root of Roman confidence,
A tree that hitherto has sheltered you
From the wild storms of Carthaginian ire,
Which menace neighbouring countries.

MASSINISSA.

                                        Scipio

She is the gentlest lady in the world,
Without a thought of strife or politics :
Domestic joys and cares engross her life ;
Her household is her universe.

SCIPIO.

                        Indeed ?
It may be so ; or else perhaps you see,
As husbands always should, with partial eyes :

So pardon bluntness from an older man
When he desires your good and speaks for Rome.

(SCIPIO *leads* MASSINISSA *to the open
door of the tent.*)

Behold within this tent, upon the right,
The bright regalia of a sovereign ;
And on the left a gentle dove, but high
Above it, perched upon a human skull,
There flaps and croaks a raven : omen dread.
Rome offers you the choice between the sides
As symbolised.

MASSINISSA (*indignantly*).

That I forsake my wife ?

SCIPIO.

Or forfeit Rome's support, and lose your throne.
Think patiently.

MASSINISSA.

But surely Rome will hold
Some other pledge of my fidelity :
Sparing me this most cruel sacrifice,
And claiming my eternal gratitude ?

SCIPIO.

Would that I might relax this exigeance !
I must obey the Senate's stern commands,

As its true bondsman, though I rule a host :
It left no other option.

MASSINISSA.

Then, alas !
If that be so I must take time to think :
And having well considered all your words,
Will send an early answer to you here,
Conveying my decision.

SCIPIO (*aside*).

No, indeed !
That has an ugly sound ; for possibly
If he returns to ponder on his course
Within the influence of his lady's charms,
He might despatch the wrong reply to me.

(*To* MASSINISSA.)

The Senate waits your final answer now,
Which I must send by special messenger ;
But let me warn you that the gods above,
Whose will I know by frequent sacrifice,
Close studying of omens, books of lore,
And converse with those skilled in augury,
Regard askance your hesitation shown ;
But if you wish for certain proof of this,
Such as is seldom granted by the gods
Except to chosen, highly-favoured men,
Torn by perplexity, proclaim aloud—
You disregard the words of Scipio.

MASSINISSA (*loudly*).

" I disregard what Scipio advocates ! "

(SCIPIO *lays his hand on the altar, and a noise as of
distant thunder in the hills is heard.*)

SCIPIO (*solemnly*).

The gods are angry : hark to Jove the king !

MASSINISSA (*uneasily*).

'Tis ominous indeed, but may be chance :
And yet how thunders thus a cloudless sky ?

(*Aside.*)

I will essay again, but dread the test.

(*Raising his voice.*)

" I disregard the words of Scipio ! "

(SCIPIO *gives the signal, and again the sound of
thunder in the mountains is heard.*)

Alas ! there is no doubt : no choice remains
For me.

SCIPIO.

You hear the voice of Jupiter,
Raised high in wrath at such perversity ;
Praise him for uttering a warning tone,
To bid you save your fortune.

MASSINISSA.

Scipio,
I thank you for your proofs of friendliness ;
Although the matter wounds me deep indeed,
And seals the mournful doom of one I love ;
For ne'er could Massinissa send his wife
To roam the world with her unguarded charms,
And tempt, like a sweet flower, the hungry bee.

(*He weeps.*)

I have no heart to commune more with you.

(*Exit* MASSINISSA.)

SCIPIO.

A sorry business, and unchivalrous,
To injure thus a gentle, lovely dame,
E'en for the vital interests of Rome.
I would the stream had run the other way !
As after victory in the Spanish wars,
I rescued my fair prisoners from all harm,
Restoring them to friends and relatives,
Who thus I gained to fight upon our side,
And, by goodwill, retained them firmly bound.
With Massinissa it was different :
I had no means to win his gratitude
And hold him longer than his whim might choose,
While stern necessity forbade delay.
If I had not persuaded him at last,
I would have had him seized within the camp,
A hostage for his countrymen's good faith ;

Or else he might have joined with Hannibal,
Instead of fighting side by side with me,
As he was pledged to do : but even now
'Tis touch and go, I hold him by a thread !

(Exit SCIPIO.)

SCENE II.

Reception-room in the palace of MASSINISSA. SOPHONISBA
seated. Enter the Hunchback.

SOPHONISBA.

Good sir, I called you, for I'm very dull,
Since absent friends have left me long at home ;
And Time, which often flies, has closed his wings,
To sleep or lag upon his track.

THE HUNCHBACK.

Madam,

In truth I willingly would do my best,
But judge the ailment difficult to cure ;
Although a jester's speech may harbour wit,
It is at best a sorry substitute
For words that might be whispered by a king.
Permit me to send Yahwa to you now :
For he has power to draw soft symphonies
From the cold metal chords that bind the lyre,
To fill the empty air with harmony.

SOPHONISBA.

A good suggestion : do so.
> (*Exit the Hunchback, and presently enter* YAHWA,
> *carrying his guitar.*)

SOPHONISBA.
> Yahwa, tune
A roundelay for me.

YAHWA.
> Madam, I pray,
What subject does your fancy indicate,
On which I may compose a melody,
With the best prospect that my muse may please ?
> (SOPHONISBA *points to a bird in a cage.*)

SOPHONISBA.
Sing of that feathered songster.

YAHWA.
> Willingly.
> (*He sings the following song.*)

SONG OF THE CAGED BIRD.
(*First come eight musical bars of the bira's song.*)

I.

I sing to you, fair mistress mine,
> And, from my playful song,
Ne'er would you deem I could repine
> Or count the hours too long.

But still my thoughts to forests turn,
    Where my wild youth was passed ;
With verdant fields and limpid burn,
    Fond memories to the last.

(*Here follow eight musical bars of the bird's song.*)

II.

With kindness fed and warmly housed,
    I pass the tranquil day ;
And view the merry throng carouse
    Or wend their joyous way.
      But still my thoughts to forests turn, &c.

(*Here follow eight musical bars of the bird's song.*)

III.

Perchance men envy me my lot
    Within this cage of gold ;
That I'm a prisoner have forgot :
    Gilt bars, like steel, can hold !
      But still my thoughts to forests turn, &c.

SOPHONISBA.

It is a sweet but melancholy strain :
Nor have I thought, with all his flood of song,
The captive might regret his woods and fields ;
But 'tis not now too late : bring here the cage,
And through the window he shall soon be free !

    (YAHWA *brings the cage :* SOPHONISBA *takes it to the*
        window and opens the door of the cage, but the
        bird does not try to escape.)

YAHWA.

He will not quit so kind a mistress ; see !
And now the little warbler sings again.
            (*Here follow eight musical bars of the bird's song.*)

IV.

Were I to seek my former home,
    All would be strange and new ;
I should regret this gilded dome,
    And grieve at leaving you !
        But still my thoughts to forests turn, &c.

SOPHONISBA.

I love the bird, and had it flown away,
It would have left a void within my heart ;
And yet I gave it liberty to go :
Indeed forced service is a thing less sweet
Than duty rendered as affection's fruit ;
And yet, perhaps, he lightly thinks of me :
By the dull force of merest habitude
Clings to the present, but regrets the past.
No, no ! he gives me proof by staying here.
Poor bird : it is not fair to doubt his love.
I thank you, Yahwa, for your song : now go,
The time is ripe for serious business.
        (*Exit* YAHWA : *then enter an Officer of the Palace.*)

OFFICER.

Madam, a messenger has come in haste,
To bring you greetings on Camilla's part.

She braved the sea, borne in a Punic barque,
And landed safely on the neighbouring coast ;
From whence she hastens, and will soon arrive
To wait upon your Highness.

SOPHONISBA.

Sir, 'tis well :
The lady is most welcome ; make it known
That I will greet her here.

OFFICER.

Madam, I will.

(*Exit Officer.*)

SOPHONISBA.

I am delighted at her quick return ;
She is a valued friend at any time,
And doubly so amid my loneliness.

(*A pause.*)

No news as yet from Massinissa's camp
Since he was summoned to meet Scipio.

(*A pause : then pettishly.*)

It is not like his use of gallantry,
As frequently he would send messengers,
Bearing no news, but compliments of love,
And seeking favours of remembrances.

(*A pause.*)

I dread such long-continued absences ;
For Sphax, who issued in full confidence,
Could meet his doom in such a little space ;
Then, if ill-fortune might accumulate,

Till every day should hatch a viper-brood
Of death, disease, mishaps, and penalties,
Such cruel reckonings would crush me soon.

(A pause.)

How gallantly the aged warrior
Bore his bold chieftainship that fatal day,
And dreamed of triumph in his kingly halls
The gods forbade he should enjoy again.
Wise is the providence that hides our fate,
And leaves to every one the boon of hope !

(Enter PARIHU.)

PARIHU.

Your Highness, now a messenger has come,
Sent by King Massinissa hurriedly ;
He begs an early audience of your Grace
In order to explain his master's wish,
And learn your answer to the King's request.

SOPHONISBA (dubiously).

What is the purport of the messages ?

PARIHU.

As yet I have not gleaned a single word :
For, madam, this strange man is reticent ;
Of sour and sombre mien, all clothed in black,
Like a dark priest of Moloch on the days
Of human sacrifice ; it seems to me
The mournful garb enshrouds a gloomier wight !

SOPHONISBA.

Admit him, and his errand shall be known
Without delay.

> (*Exit* PARIHU, *who returns with the Messenger,
> and then withdraws to a little distance. The
> Messenger approaches* SOPHONISBA *and bends
> low before her ; he then stands erect and silent,
> waiting for her to speak, and holding in his
> hand a small casket.*)

SOPHONISBA.

What tidings from my liege ?

MESSENGER.

Your Highness, if I had my earnest wish,
I would have shunned this painful embassy ;
Though proud to render humble services
In any way.

SOPHONISBA (*anxiously*).

Say quickly how it lies ?

MESSENGER.

Great Scipio has quarrelled with the King,
Because he wed the daughter of a foe,
Linking himself with enemies of Rome.

SOPHONISBA.

But surely, when 'tis known that I avoid
The stormy ocean men call politics,
And only seek to give my husband peace,
Then Rome could not behold offence in me?

MESSENGER.

I would it were so, madam ; but, alas,
Scipio has spoken !

SOPHONISBA (*proudly*).

     Pray remember, sir.
Here Massinissa rules, not Scipio !

MESSENGER.

Madam, the King has sent a lethal cup,
   (*He takes a metal cup out of the case which he is
    holding, and unscrews the lid.*)
And bids you drink it for the country's sake ;
   (SOPHONISBA *buries her face in her hands
    with a gesture of despair.*)
Which soon must perish, left without allies,
Under the iron heel of Punic might,
Or else be seized by Rome victorious.
He bids a sad farewell, and prays you act
With the high courage of your warrior race ;
Worthy of them, and worthy of yourself—
Wife of two kings of Africa !

(SOPHONISBA *recovers herself ; she makes a gesture to the Messenger to withdraw a little, and he retires to the background, where he stands with his black cloth head-dress, which is bound round his head, drawn across his face so as almost to conceal it entirely, except the eyes.*)

SOPHONISBA (*aside*).

Alas !
Doomed by my husband, why then longer live
When all that made life happy has decayed ?
I might escape ; but who would rescue me
From being captured and brought back again ?
Of all my kin, alone my mother lives :
But she is old and powerless to protect.

(PARIHU *respectfully approaches* SOPHONISBA.)

PARIHU.

Your Highness, pardon me as one of years
Spent in the faithful service of King Sphax,
Whose spirit prompts me now to offer you
Such counsel as may lie within my power,
To meet the troubles that assail your Grace ;
And stand revealed, in spite of all disguise,
To one who has seen many a turn of fate
In good or evil fortune.

SOPHONISBA.

Parihu,
I thank you most sincerely for your words,

But I cannot disclose the evil news
Which suddenly has overwhelmed me.

PARIHU.

No :
I would not press you to declare the cause,
As you desire to guard its secresy ;
But if by chance you should have need of me—
Believe it no mere vaunting when I say—
My arm though old has not quite lost its power
To wield the sword it bore in many a fight ;
Nor have I yet forgot the art of war ;
And if your Highness were in danger now,
Whoever he might be that threatens you,
Speak but one word and all the realm shall rise
And guard your safety with its dearest blood ;
Even to place you on a single throne,
And conquer freedom for our state again,
So lately lost when Sphax's power succumbed
Through over-confidence.

SOPHONISBA.

Excuse me, sir :
I'm somewhat hard of hearing, and my ear
Does not record your words.   You may withdraw.

(*Exit* PARIHU, *after bowing*.   SOPHONISBA
soliloquises.)

His duty or ambition bade him give
Desperate advice in desperate circumstance ;

But I will never plunge the realm in blood
And bring upon it miseries untold ;
Nor would I quit the honourable path
That I have strictly followed through my life,
And seek salvation in rebellion.
My husband bids me immolate myself,
To save our subjects from the injury
Wrought by my marriage, unawares to me,
Which tempts the Romans to abandon them
To suffer servitude, rapine, and death ;
And I alone have power to rescue them.
Both wifely instinct prompts me to obey,
And queenly duty bids the sacrifice :
My father's blood, which thrills through all my veins,
Impels and nerves me to the noble deed !

(*A pause.*)

Shall I await Camilla's coming?   No :
For she might shake my rightly-formed resolve.
What parting message shall I send the King ?

(*She draws herself to her full height, and,
turning, addresses the Messenger.*)

Bring here the cup, and tell my lord the King
That when I drained it thus I spoke of him :—
My death seems to be following somewhat close
Upon my wedding to his majesty !

(*The Messenger, who has approached, hands her the
cup : she drinks and dies.   Exit the Messenger.
Presently enter an Officer conducting* KATHARNA ;
the Officer hurries to the prostrate form of
SOPHONISBA.)

OFFICER.

Alas, the Queen !

KATHARNA.

What new catastrophe ?

OFFICER.

She's dead ! I'll call for help.

(*Exit Officer, hurriedly.*)

KATHARNA.

Ill-fated day
When first I urged her on to wed with Sphax
And quit her peaceful Carthaginian home !

(*A pause.*)

Alas, alas, she's gone ! My friend, who bore
The fairest face : the gentlest, truest heart,
That ever warmed for me and was unchanged.

(KATHARNA *weeps. Re-enter the Officer with*
the Messenger of the King.)

OFFICER.

This man was latest with her majesty,
And gained an audience as a messenger
Sent by King Massinissa.

KATHARNA (*to the Messenger*).

Sir, explain :
What know you of our lady's death ?

MESSENGER.

Madam,
The King commissioned me to bring her doom
Within this cup ; and she drank willingly :
His marriage caused mistrust of him at Rome,
And as he had wed a Carthaginian dame
Within whose veins there flowed a warrior's blood.
Here is my warrant and the royal seal.

(*He draws from his bosom a parchment : unfolds
and holds it, offering it for the inspection of
KATHARNA and the Officer ; the latter takes it,
and scrutinises it with signs of astonishment.
The Officer and Messenger withdraw to one
side, and appear to discuss the document for a
moment or two ; the Officer then hurries out as
if to call assistance, and the Messenger follows
him slowly.*)

KATHARNA (*soliloquises*).

Alas ! that all the vines I plant with care
Are killed by failure's cold and blackening frost,
Before they bear the fruit, yielding the wine
To slake my thirst for vengeance on fell Rome !
But this was one of fortune's cruellest blows ;
For look beneath the surface of events,
And note how narrow was the turning-point
Where Sophonisba chose between the two :
Whether to die or triumph after all.
She might have saved herself and won the day,

Holding the country for the Punic cause ;
Freeing it rightly from a miscreant,
Who by his treachery and cowardice
Had proved unworthy of his throne and her ;
Although it needed desperate device,
And recklessness to human suffering,
To win the country in such threatening straits ;
No less than to rebel and raise the torch,
Setting this peaceful kingdom in a blaze :
Bringing the misery of civil war
Upon a country that she died to save.
The plan would not occur to one so kind,
Or, coming to the mind, be cast aside ;
And yet it promised richly for success :
The state was ready for the smallest spark
To fire the train its recent conquest laid ;
And all within it longed to burst the chains
That Massinissa had so lately bound,
Making the great the captive of the small.
Ah ! if I had arrived but yesterday,
And not a day too late, it had been done !
But grief is useless and a waste of time :
Yet, to atone for Sophonisba's blood—

                                    (*A pause.*)

Alas ! I fear it is beyond my power,
And must be left to time and Nemesis.
But I have business calling me away :
No dainty dallying with needlework,
Or tuning softly to a passing whim
Upon the blithe guitar that once I loved.
            (*She speaks faster, from excitement.*)

At least I scorn to send my friends to death
And hide myself in base security ;
The fateful battle still impends between
The hosts of Hannibal and Scipio :

(*Raising her voice, from enthusiastic excitement.*)

There will I hie ; and on my Roman foe,
E'en with a woman's hand, will draw the bow !

(*She raises her hand in the air, and rushes
out. Curtain.*)

SCENE III.

*A grove upon the plain of Zama, midway between the
Roman and Carthaginian camp. Enter* HANNIBAL
and GISCO.

HANNIBAL.

It would have proved a wiser plan for us
Had I remained to fight in Italy,
Allowing Scipio to waste his strength
Against our massive walls, behind whose crest
The citizens, unwarlike and unskilled,
Would have been better suited to defence
Than in the open against well-trained troops :
But Carthage ordered, and I have obeyed.
Now if I can postpone the battle hour,
Gaining more time in which to drill the men,
It would be in our favour ; so I sought

This interview, in which to try my power :
Whether I may cajole or bribe the foe,
To yield part of the vantage that he holds
Through being ready earlier than we.
But here is Scipio—

(*Enter* SCIPIO, *attended by an Officer.*)

Welcome, general ;
Renowned for courteous enlightenment !

SCIPIO.

I greet you, Hannibal, of world-wide fame
For martial deeds.

HANNIBAL.

Shall we converse alone ?

SCIPIO.

If you prefer it.

HANNIBAL.

Certainly I do :
Go, Gisco, to my escort ; bid it wait
Upon the border of the wood.

GISCO.

Yes, sir.

(*Exit* GISCO.)

SCIPIO (*to his Officer*).

Pray join the guard : I will return alone,
After this meeting.

ROMAN OFFICER.

Yes, your Excellency.

(*Exit Officer.*)

HANNIBAL.

I am a man whose trade is war, not words,
So pardon my simplicity of speech.
Here stand our mighty nations face to face :
Why should two lions fight, not share the spoil?
Let us divide the world between our powers,
But live henceforth in peace and amity.
We recognise your sovereignty in Spain,
Sardinia, Sicily, and Italy :
The rest remains for us beyond your sphere
Of action.

SCIPIO.

Sir, I have no power to treat,
Much less conclude, a compact which requires
The Senate's seal.

HANNIBAL.

Then send a messenger,
Reporting the fair offers which I make,
And asking a decision.

SCIPIO.

No, my lord ;
It would need time, and in the interim
Your skilful preparations march apace,
And your untrained recruits might learn their trade.

HANNIBAL.

What matters that, if the result be peace ?
You benefit your country and my own,
Stirring with patriotic gratitude
The heart of one who lives to serve her cause :
In recognising this, name but the gift,
For I possess the power to richly grant.
So if your wishes lie within its range,
To ask is to receive.

SCIPIO (*turning away*).

Enough, enough !
For honour bids me to decline at once,

(*A pause.*)

Though I perforce must pardon you the words :
Knowing your stress of patriotic zeal
And dire necessity.

HANNIBAL.

I thank you, sir,
For your forbearance ; I meant no offence.
Think well of our alliance while there's time,

And what you risk if you encounter us ;
My troops will fight like furies, for they guard
Their city, families, their fame and wealth.

SCIPIO.

We have discussed the matter fully, sir.

HANNIBAL.

Can you propose more fitting terms ?

SCIPIO.

My lord,
I know the warlike skill of Hannibal,
But Carthaginians are unused to arms :
There are no means by which we could agree.

HANNIBAL (*impatiently*).

Time presses, sir ; adieu !

SCIPIO (*coldly*).

My lord, adieu !
(*Exit* HANNIBAL.)

SCIPIO.

Hear everything—say little as may be ;
That is the plan for generals in the field.
Although he did not learn much from my words,
He told me nothing that I did not know.
(*Exit* SCIPIO.)

SCENE IV.

The public gardens at Carthage. Enter HERCTA
followed by MUTHUMBAL.

HERCTA.

Come quickly, dearest !

MUTHUMBAL (*playfully*).

It is easy said ;
But I am not so light and fleet of foot
As in old days when I ran after you,
A happy youth in Spain.

HERCTA.

Well, well, my dear,
'Tis an advantage surely that you wed
With a young wife, who fills you with new life !

MUTHUMBAL.

Then she returns my constant compliments.

HERCTA.

I would 'twere possible I could enjoy
This happiness without uneasiness
For my dear mistress ; but at last there comes
Katharna's messenger !

MUTHUMBAL.

I hope he brings
Good news this time.

(Enter a Messenger.)

MESSENGER *(to* HERCTA).

Madam, well met indeed !
I come from Dame Katharna with her love
And kindly greetings, besides messages :
That on Queen Sophonisba's sudden death
She journeyed forth to join the Punic host
About to close in fight with Scipio.
If victory crown its efforts, then all's well,
And she will soon return, meeting you here,
To dwell in Carthage.

HERCTA.

But where will she go
In case defeat should overtake our troops,
Which may the gods forbid !

MESSENGER.

She did not say,
In that event, how she would save herself :
Katharna spoke the few and simple words
That I have mentioned.   Now I must return
To join my lady on the battlefield.

She follows near the archers of the guard ;
In her magician's dress remains unknown,
Unhindered, and unhelped.

HERCTA.

     I'll go with you,
If, dear Muthumbal, you will give me leave.
I might be useful to my lady there,
And even yet persuade her to return
Here, safe within these walls.

MESSENGER.

     Consider well :
'Tis a rough journey for a woman, though,
And dangers of worst kinds beset the path
Of her who wanders near a battlefield,
Where fate decides which way the tide shall flow
That may engulf her in its struggling waves :
So pause ere you adventure.

HERCTA.

     Thank you, sir,
For all your information and advice ;
I heed no risk. Muthumbal, may I go ?

MUTHUMBAL.

I will not offer any obstacle
To what you wish to do in faithfulness ;

But rather will myself accompany you,
So that you may not lack ready defence
In case of difficulty.

HERCTA.

Then you earn
My deepest gratitude.

MESSENGER.

Let it be so ;
If you have both determined, we will start
After the shortest possible delay.
Thus we may reach the Carthaginian host
To-morrow evening ere the sun be set :
Though before then the battle may be fought
For which the armies gathered on the plains
Of Zama.

HERCTA.

Sir, we cannot go too soon.
My preparations will be quickly made ;
And yours, Muthumbal ?

MUTHUMBAL.

All within an hour.

(*Exeunt.*)

SCENE V.

*A road leading from the field of Zama towards Carthage :
immediately after the battle, and overthrow of the
Carthaginians. Enter* KATHARNA, *wounded, from
the battlefield. She wears her magician's dress, and
carries a bow in her hand, with a quiver of arrows
slung over her shoulder.*

KATHARNA.

Like a spent arrow I have sped my course.

(*She staggers and sinks upon the ground in a swoon
Enter* HANNIBAL *and* GISCO *from the battlefield.*)

HANNIBAL.

Our walls must answer for the victory now ;
As Scipio failed to capture Utica,
So Carthage must resist and may escape.
Then word has come from bold Antiochus
That he collects his troops to lend us aid.
But who lies here ? a female warrior
So sorely wounded in our country's cause ?
(He approaches KATHARNA.)
It seems this flow of blood foretells her doom.
I now recall that we met recently,
As I was passing to the Senate-house,
And I was influenced by her eloquence.
Her sayings blazed with patriotic fire

When she expressed her hopes of victory
For Carthage, Afric's champion against Rome.
And though the well-mouthed solemn babblings
Of augurs, wizards, witches, all the crew,
Move me but little by their drolleries,
She hinted matters which impressed my mind
With a vague feeling that she knew far more
Than what she said : unlike the rest of them,
Who blab on hazard more than they can know.
And further, it appeared her voice and mien
Recalled the past to me—as some old tune
Revives the memories of the days gone by.

(A pause.)

But duty bids that we should hurry on,
Nor lose the precious moments longer.
> (HANNIBAL *is about to turn away when he observes*
> *and recognises the ring on* KATHARNA'S *finger.*)

HANNIBAL (*starting forwara*).

Ha !

My ring ! Katharna ! what a dreadful fate !

(Aside.)

Oh, cruel Gavius, had you ne'er been born !
How different had all been but for your crime !
> (KATHARNA *opens her eyes and gazes at* HANNIBAL.)

KATHARNA.

O Hannibal, my only love ! Alas !

(She smiles faintly.)

My evening star that heralds coming night.

HANNIBAL (*passionately*).

Would I might die, and so remain with you !

(*A pause.*)

The sacred cause of Carthage claims of me
That I must live and serve it.   Tell me, love,
Why did you not make yourself known to me
So lately in the garden where we met ?
For then I could have shielded you from harm,
And still before us now there might have beamed
A bright and constant ray of happiness,
Cheering us on our road, howe'er beset :
But now the evil work is done !

KATHARNA.

Forgive,
Forgive me, Hannibal !   Indeed I feared
Our love would rise like some wild stream in flood,
Sweeping before it every obstacle,
Engulfing in oblivion all our cares
And our stern duties in the present war.

(*A pause.*)

Fast ebbing strength forbids me to disclose
More of my life since first I quitted Spain ;
And yet a word will tell its chief success.
My influence sent Hasdrubal to your aid ;
I ever sought your interests, be assured.
When I am gone, seek faithful Hercta's help
At her new home within the city's bounds ;
She wed Muthumbal, scribe to Malchus, there,

And will explain to you my works and ends,
My wanderings, and efforts in the cause ;
But for this wound I would still serve it more,
And even yet, perhaps——

> (*She partly raises herself, but sinks back exhausted,
> and after a pause resumes faintly.*)

No, no—too late.

> (*A pause after which she continues : raising her
> hand towards the sky, and following its direction
> intently with her gaze.*)

Father, accept the offerings that I bring.

> (HANNIBAL *and* GISCO *respectfully withdraw a little,
> and* HANNIBAL *turns partly away to conceal his
> grief.* KATHARNA *continues.*)

Though Rome may rue the deeds of Gavius,
Enough of Roman blood has not been shed
To soothe your manes and give your spirit rest :
Take mine ! Take mine !

> (*Raising herself a little, she tears open her wound.*)

GISCO (*springing forward to prevent her*).

No, no—too late.

Stop ! stop !

HANNIBAL (*turning towards them*).

'Tis done !

KATHARNA (*sinking down*).

Take mine !

(HANNIBAL *hastens to her and finds her dead.*
Enter HERCTA, MUTHUMBAL, *and the Messenger.*
HERCTA *hurries to* KATHARNA.)

HANNIBAL.

Truly a deity in a woman's form.
Empires might draw life from her sunny smiles ;
Whole nations reeled, thrones tottered at her frown !

(*Curtain.*)

THE END.

www.ingramcontent.com/pod-product-compliance
Lightning Source LLC
Chambersburg PA
CBHW030837270326
41928CB00007B/1101